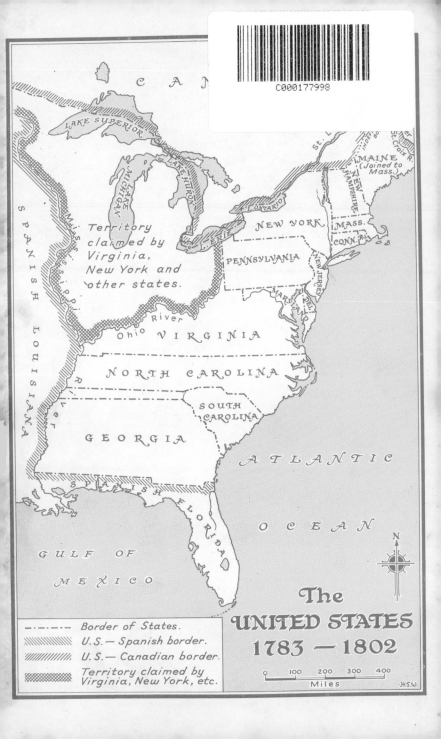

C000177998

CANADA

LAKE SUPERIOR

LAKE MICHIGAN

LAKE HURON

L. ONTARIO

L. ERIE

Territory claimed by Virginia, New York and other states.

Mississippi River

SPANISH LOUISIANA

Ohio River

VIRGINIA

NORTH CAROLINA

SOUTH CAROLINA

GEORGIA

NEW YORK

PENNSYLVANIA

MASS.

CONN. R.I.

NEW JERSEY

MD.

DEL.

MAINE (Joined to Mass.)

NEW HAMPSHIRE

St. Croix R.

VT.

St. L.

ATLANTIC OCEAN

SPANISH FLORIDA

GULF OF MEXICO

N

The
UNITED STATES
1783 — 1802

–·–·– Border of States.
▨▨▨ U.S. — Spanish border.
▨▨▨ U.S. — Canadian border.
▨▨▨ Territory claimed by Virginia, New York, etc.

0   100   200   300   400
Miles

H.S.W.

THEN AND THERE SERIES
GENERAL EDITOR
MARJORIE REEVES, M.A., PH.D.

The American Revolution
(1775 - 1783)

CLORINDA CLARKE

Illustrated from contemporary sources by

H. TOOTHILL and **H. S. WHITHORNE**

LONGMAN

LONGMAN GROUP LIMITED
London

*Associated companies, branches and representatives
throughout the world*

*First published 1964
Seventh impression 1974*

ISBN 0 582 20398 8

ACKNOWLEDGEMENTS

The maps are based on those in *Atlas of American
History* by James Truslow Adams. Copyright 1943
Charles Scribner's Sons.

*Printed in Hong Kong by
Sheck Wah Tong Printing Press*

CONTENTS

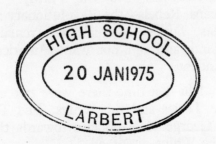

TO THE READER

The American Revolution, the longest war America has ever fought, lasted eight years. In so small a book I cannot mention all of its generals, battles, or even campaigns. But I have tried to include the ones that seem to me to have had the greatest influence on the Revolution's outcome—American independence.

I grew up in the centre of New York State, not far from the Oriskany Battlefield. As a little girl I visited General Herkimer's big, red house. I hunted Indian arrowheads in the ravine where the Indians ambushed the Americans. Some day I hope you will visit my country and see these and many other landmarks of our Revolution.

I am, also, one of the many Americans whose ancestors fought in the Revolution. (My father's family were Loyalist, my mother's, Rebel.)

All armies have many names for themselves and their enemies. The American Revolutionary soldier was no different, but in this book I use only a few of these names:

   British, Redcoats—the King's army
   Americans, Rebels—the Revolutionary Army
   Loyalists, Tories—colonials who remained loyal to
      England and did not want America to be in-
      dependent.

In England, at that time there were two chief political parties—the Tories and the Whigs. The Tories agreed with King George III's policies towards the American colonies. The Whigs disagreed.

No Tax, No Tea

Rally Mohawks! Bring out your axes.
And tell King George we'll pay no taxes.

Two hundred men, their faces stained with soot, marched through the streets of Boston in the colony of Massachusetts. They were wrapped in Indian blankets and carried tomahawks and hatchets. It was six o'clock in the evening, 16 December 1773.

On reaching a wharf in Boston Harbour, they divided into three groups and boarded three ships. From the holds they hauled over 300 chests of tea, split them open and dumped them into the black water.

'And all the while we were surrounded by British ships. But no attempt was made to resist us,' wrote one of the 'Indians', sixty years later.

It was not until 1775 that the first battles of the American Revolution were fought, but with the Boston Tea Party, the Revolution began.

The American Revolution did not start as a war for independence. During its first year, no Americans said they wanted to leave the British Empire. What they wanted was the restoration of their 'Englishmen's rights' within the Empire. These rights King George III and his government threatened. Not until after July 1776, when the Americans had tried and tried to explain how they felt to the King, and he had refused to listen, did they declare independence.

King George III in his coronation robes

Since 1607, for over 150 years, Englishmen had crossed
the Atlantic and started new colonies on the east coast of
North America. By 1773, the year of the Boston Tea
Party, there were thirteen such colonies, as you can see
on the first map inside the front cover. But by 1773, also,
not all the colonists were of English origin. There were
also Scots, Irish, Dutch, French Huguenots, Germans,
Swedes and Swiss. They brought ideas and customs of
their own, and mixed them with the English ones.

During the first 150 years of the American colonies, the government in England paid little attention to them. The colonists were allowed to develop their own life and laws—many of them, naturally, quite different from the life and laws that were developing back in England.

Though the colonies became different from the English politically, they still fought for her. Whenever England had a war with France, Holland or Spain in Europe, the colonies fought her enemies in America. The last of these wars they called the French and Indian War. (It was part of the Seven Years War which lasted from 1756 to 1763.)

The treaty that ended that war in 1763 had a tremendous effect on the whole British Empire—particularly in America. In it France gave up her vast lands in Canada to England. Spain gave up Florida to England. British rule in America stretched from north to south, from the Atlantic to the Mississippi except for one city, New Orleans, at the very south.

The Americans were no longer afraid of French invasion from Canada, and so many no longer felt the need for English protection. On the other hand the government in England felt, with this new enormous empire, they could no longer rule their colonies in the old, easy, lax way.

So in 1764 Parliament started to pass new laws and to enforce old ones that had been forgotten. These laws affected the colonies' trade, their rights to move westward into Indian country, their churches, their financial responsibility for the British Army on their soil and their taxes.

Taxation was a particularly sore point. The French and Indian War had cost the British a huge sum and their debts were heavy. King George III decided the colonies should be taxed to help pay this debt, and also to pay towards future defence of the American frontier.

3

Lord Chatham

Now from the beginning, though the colonies recognized the King's authority in some things, they did not recognize his right to make them pay taxes they had not voted for. Lord Chatham, a former British Prime Minister and a warm friend of the colonies, put it this way: 'No subject of England shall be taxed but by his own consent.'

The colonies meant the same thing when they cried: 'No taxation without representation.'

But the British Government insisted. Taxes were put on sugar, silk, calico and wine. The Stamp Act, passed in 1765, declared that no document was legal unless it carried a government-issued stamp. All American *imports** and *exports* had to travel in British ships.

As more and more of these taxes were imposed the colonists grew angrier and angrier. They complained. They rioted. They

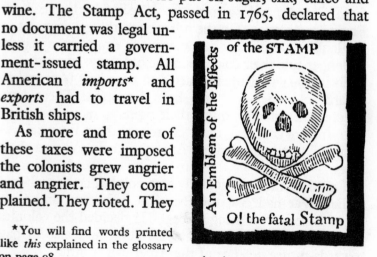

An Emblem of the Effects of the STAMP

O! the fatal Stamp

American cartoon on the Stamp Act

*You will find words printed like *this* explained in the glossary on page 98.

4

attacked the homes of British officials in America. Finally, they refused to buy any of the taxed articles from England.

When the British merchants began to lose more money in lost trade than the government made in taxes, they criticized the taxes too. Gradually many of them were removed.

Then in 1773 Parliament declared a new tax—a tax on tea. The colonists protested. They said no tea was to land in their ports, and if it were landed it would be put in warehouses and not sold. In Boston alone the authorities refused to take any notice of the colonists' protests.

That is why those Boston men dressed up as Indians, masked themselves with black soot and dumped the tea into Boston Harbour—£18,000 sterling worth of tea!

The British Government was now very angry. One Member of Parliament said the people of Boston 'ought to be knocked about their ears and destroyed'.

As punishment, Parliament passed the *Coercive Acts*. (Colonists called them the *Intolerable Acts*.) The government of Massachusetts lost many of its liberties. The capital was moved from Boston to Salem. Town meetings were restricted. Boston Harbour was closed to all shipping, even ferry-boats. A military governor, General Thomas Gage, was sent out from England.

Edmund Burke

5

His orders were to restore none of Boston's freedoms until the £18,000 sterling worth of tea was paid for.

Many Englishmen were shocked by this harshness, especially members of the *Whig* party, such as the former Prime Minister, Lord Chatham, Edmund Burke, the Irish *orator*, and Charles James Fox.

Boston had sympathizers in many other American colonies. When the Boston Port Bill (closing Boston Harbour) came into effect in June 1774, they sent food and supplies to the Bostonians. Virginia sent Indian corn; Maryland, pork, rye and bread; New Hampshire, cows and money.

The TIMES are
Dreadful,
Dismal
Doleful
Dolorous, and
DOLLAR-LESS.

From the Pennsylvania Journal, 1765

People on both sides of the Atlantic were amazed. Until now the colonies had rarely agreed on anything and were jealous and distrustful of one another. King George and his ministers had never dreamt that the other twelve colonies would rally behind Massachusetts against the Crown.

One reason for this widespread support was the growth of Committees of Correspondence. A Massachusetts Rebel, Sam Adams, had founded them in 1772. He set up a system of letter-writers and post-riders. Whenever the British did anything that annoyed the local Rebels, the Committees wrote long letters about it and sent them racing to the other cities, and correspondents in all the colonies. This constant exchange of news did much to keep the revolutionary spirit alive and organize opposition

6

to the new laws. It was their substitute for telegraph and radio!

Also, in every colony, revolutionary parliaments called *Provincial Congresses* were set up. The colony of Virginia, second only to Massachusetts in revolutionary zeal, urged large annual meetings of *delegates* from all of the Congresses.

So, in September 1774, the delegates to the First *Continental Congress* met. They met in the largest city in America, and the second largest in the British Empire, Philadelphia, in Pennsylvania colony.

Every colony was represented at the First Continental Congress except Georgia. Virginia sent a stately army officer and landowner, George Washington. From Pennsylvania came an old astute *diplomat* and inventor, Benjamin Franklin. Sam Adams and his cousin John, the lawyer, represented Massachusetts.

The Provincial Congresses also reorganized the *militia*, or local bands of volunteer soldiers in each colony. They got rid of any officer who did not agree with them politically. They started companies of young, very active soldiers called Minute Men. (Named so because they could spring to arms in a minute.)

The Provincial Congresses also ordered that ammunition and supplies be collected and stored in places of safety. Massachusetts' largest depot was in Concord, a town about eighteen miles from Boston. There the New England Rebels hid axes, medicine, gunpowder, candles, wine and raisins, all important to eighteenth-century warfare.

Boston's Battlefields

When General Thomas Gage, the new military governor, arrived in Boston on 13 May 1774, he hoped he was coming as a peacemaker. He had lived for eighteen years in the colonies, had an American wife, and was a Whig who had long disapproved of the King's policies towards his American subjects. But he did not understand one of the most important changes resulting from the French and Indian War. Since the French were no longer in Canada to threaten them, the Massachusetts men were beginning

Boston in peacetime

to feel that they no longer needed England for protection. This made them all the more ready to oppose restrictions.

Before he left England, Gage had told the government that he was sure 1,500 soldiers were all he would need to restore order. After one summer of trying to rule the resentful Bostonians, he sent back a different message. If the government thought they should send 10,000 men, they had better send 20,000! If they had planned on giving him one million pounds, to make it two!

But he got little support from the King and his advisers. They disagreed completely among themselves. The King was for severity. Lord North, his Prime Minister, wanted to make peace.

So Gage kept on grimly in Boston, trying to maintain order. He could not do much but his spies told him about the ammunition and other supplies growing daily in Concord. They, at least, could be destroyed. Under cover of night, on 18 April 1775, he sent six British companies out from Boston towards Concord.

But the Rebels had spies in it, too. One of the most active was a gifted silversmith named Paul Revere. He was also one of the post-riders who carried letters for the Committees of Correspondence.

When the Rebel leaders heard that Gage's troops were on the move, they suspected that Concord was in danger. They were also worried lest the British would capture, in near-by Lexington, two leading Boston revolutionaries, old Sam Adams, and the rich young John Hancock. They asked Paul Revere and a friend of his, William Dawes, to spread a warning throughout the countryside.

Both men carried the message, but because Henry Wadsworth Longfellow, a New England poet, wrote a long poem in 1863 about Paul Revere, he is far more famous than Dawes.

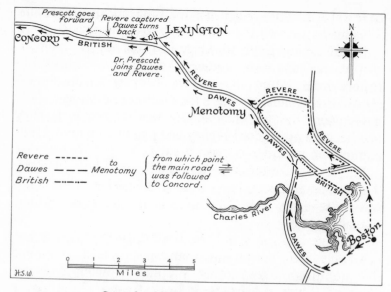

Concord and Lexington April 18–19, 1775

Revere was rowed across the Charles River, borrowed a horse and then by moonlight set out at a gallop on the road towards Lexington. Dodging British patrols, he reached Lexington, alarming 'almost every house' on the way. Adams and Hancock were warned of their danger. Then Dawes, Revere, and a Dr Prescott, who was out late courting his girl, started for Concord with the news 'The *redcoats* are coming!'

Revere was captured by a patrol and was being taken back to Boston when he escaped, lost his horse, and made his way to safety on foot.

As a post-rider for Committees of Correspondence, Revere was to carry many important messages all through the Revolution, but none was more important or famous than the one he carried from Boston to Lexington that night. He may have lost the horse, but the Minute Men were warned. When, early next morning, the six companies of redcoats marched on to Lexington Green a band of armed and determined farmers was there to meet them.

'Disperse, ye rebels,' ordered Major John Pitcairn, the British commanding officer. A gun went off. No one knows for sure to this day who fired the first shot of the American Revolution, an English soldier or an American farmer. Both sides had been strictly ordered not to shoot.

Eight of the American militia died in the gunfire that followed, ten were wounded. The rest scattered. The British companies marched on to Concord. They destroyed whatever supplies had not already been hidden away by Americans.

Then the weary march back to Boston began. From behind every rock, tree and wall, American farmers shot at the British soldiers. By the time the troops reached the city, 273 men out of a redcoat force of 1,800 had fallen.

For several years now the Rebel *agitators* had been organizing the Sons of Liberty in most of the towns and cities. They were groups of men and boys, who used any new British tax law or regulation as an excuse to riot and attack the homes of British officials and those who sided with the government.

When the Massachusetts Committee of Correspondence sent word of the doings at Lexington and Concord through the colonies, blaming the British for firing first, whether they did or not, the Sons of Liberty ran rampant. They stormed the houses of people on the British side, tarring and feathering the owners. They threatened the British governors who fled from them to British warships. Volunteer soldiers from all over New England hurried towards the Rebel camp outside Boston. Soon the city was under a nine-mile-long siege.

Early in May the New Englanders struck in another

direction. Near the Canadian border, at Ticonderoga, between Lake George and Lake Champlain, there was a tumbledown fort.

A band of outlaws under a giant leader, Ethan Allen (they called themselves the Green Mountain Boys from their home in the Green Mountains of New Hampshire) set out to capture Fort Ticonderoga. On the way Allen was joined by a fiery, energetic Connecticut *apothecary*, turned army captain, Benedict Arnold.

Allen's Green Mountain Boys captured the forty-five redcoats in Ticonderoga 'In the name of the Great Jehovah and the Continental Congress', surprising them while they slept.

With Ticonderoga the Americans had gained an important *strategic point* on the road to Canada. Better still, they captured sorely-needed cannon. These were the guns that the following December Washington was to send north for—guns that in March 1776 forced the British to give up Boston.

Late in May General Gage's long-awaited reinforcements reached Boston—6,600 men under three British generals: Sir William Howe, Sir Henry Clinton, and John Burgoyne.

Howe and Clinton knew the colonies well. Howe had fought in the French and Indian War. He was a Whig who had been re-elected to Parliament in 1774, on the promise that he would refuse any command against the American colonists. But when orders came to go to Boston to oppose the Rebels he obeyed, like a good soldier.

Sir Henry Clinton had grown up in New York City where his father had been governor for ten years. Burgoyne was a good soldier but also a great dandy. His troops called him Gentleman Johnny.

All three generals arrived in Boston eager to end the

siege. Their plan was to fortify some of the heights surrounding the city. However, General Artemas Ward, elderly commander of the New England troops, got wind of the plan and moved first.

Two small hills rose on the Charleston peninsula near Boston. General Ward ordered that the taller one, Bunker Hill, should be fortified. But it was on the smaller, Breed's Hill, that Colonel William Prescott's men built their *redoubt*. They had gone out after dark and worked all through the night building the fort.

Next morning Boston was dumbfounded. The evening before, Breed's Hill had been empty. Now it had earthworks alive with digging soldiers.

There is a story that General Gage sent for one of his Loyalist councillors, Abijah Willard. He pointed to the hill. 'Do you know that tall man on the parapet?' he asked.

Willard peered through the general's spy glass. 'It is Colonel William Prescott, my brother-in-law.'

'Will he fight?'

'I cannot answer for his men, but he will fight you to the gates of Hell.'

'The fort must be captured!' General Gage said firmly.

Prescott had chosen a place that could have been cut off easily, if British troops had landed behind it.

But the professional soldiers in Gage's council simply couldn't believe that raw, untrained farmers would stand up to a head-on attack from British regulars.

So in the mid-afternoon of 17 June, led by General Howe himself, the British regiments, sweating under heavy packs, toiled in slow march up the hill directly facing the fort.

An order had been given the Rebels: 'Don't fire until you see the whites of their eyes.' So they waited.

When the British were only fifty yards away the Rebels

fired. Twice the redcoat lines broke and were driven back, leaving piles of wounded and dead. When they returned the third time, the Americans had no more gunpowder. 'Their fire went out like an old candle.' The British took the fort with a bayonet charge, the retreating Americans wielding their musket butts like clubs.

Howe had succeeded in capturing Breed's Hill but at the cost of 1,000 killed or wounded. The Americans lost only 400—and one alone was from Boston.

Back in England there was horror at the size of the

George Washington

British losses. Sir William Eden told the Prime Minister, 'Eight more such victories and we shall have no one left to report them.'

The Battle of Bunker Hill (the name it was given although it was fought over Breed's Hill) showed that untrained militia could stand up to trained soldiers. General Howe always remembered Bunker Hill's slaughter with such bitterness that although personally a very brave man and a fine strategist, he never again would attack an American fortified position. Though he won many battles he never followed them up, but delayed until his enemy could slip away. No one knows why—natural laziness or Whig sympathies? But possibly it was because Howe behaved like this that Britain lost her American colonies.

After Bunker Hill, Gage made

14

no more attempts against the besieging New Englanders. This may be because of the great casualties he had suffered. He might well have succeeded if he had tried. The New England Army was disorganized, undisciplined, low in ammunition—and dwindling from desertions.

On 14 June the Second Continental Congress, then sitting in Philadelphia, took a momentous step. It adopted the New England Army outside of Boston. The day after it named a commander for the army. He was George Washington, a Virginia gentleman, *veteran* of the French and Indian War and one of its own members. He was on horseback, on his way to Massachusetts to take over his new post, when he got the news of the Battle of Bunker Hill.

The main reason Congress chose Washington was a political one—he came from Virginia. Congress, however, could not have selected better. Not that it seemed so at first. At first, Washington made some almost fatal mistakes—but he learned from those mistakes.

As the Revolution dragged on year after year, Washington held together a hungry, ragged army, controlled jealous generals, coped with a stingy Congress. Most important—when he realized that he could never beat the British forces in America without the help of sea power, he refused to risk his small army in unnecessary battles until the French navy was on hand to help him. Unlike the generals opposing him, Washington saw just what he had to do to win the Revolution. When after six years of setbacks, his chance for a decisive victory came, he seized it.

Britain loses Boston but keeps Canada

When George Washington took over the forces surrounding Boston, he was disgusted by what he found. There was filth, disorder, little discipline, ammunition or supplies. He wrote his cousin, Lund, 'They are an exceedingly dirty and nasty people,' and set out sternly, with *pillory* and lash, to make soldiers of them.

Washington was convinced of the justice of the American position. He wrote to a friend, who was fearful at the way things were going, 'I think the Parliament of Great Britain hath no more right to put their hands into my pocket, without my consent, than I have to put my hands into yours for money.'

At the same time, he was one of the many Americans who blamed the Parliament and not the King for the troubles of the colonies. He was so sure at that time that the King would soon listen to his American subjects' complaints, that he wrote his wife, Martha, 'I shall return safe to you in the fall [the autumn].'

But summer wore on into autumn, and autumn into winter. Sir William Howe inside Boston did nothing to break the siege, but neither did the Ministers in England seem ready to try to settle the dispute. In December, with most of his army threatening to go home when their *enlistments* ran out on the thirty-first, Washington thought of the great cannon that had been captured at Ticonderoga.

He promoted a fat young bookseller from Boston, Henry Knox, to Chief of Engineers, and sent him off to Ticonderoga to get the fifty guns. It was a tremendous job. The cannon had to be floated down Lake George and carried on sledges nearly 300 miles through the snowy New England mountains. It was almost February before the cannon reached Washington's headquarters. And when they came lumbering into camp there was not enough gunpowder for a full-scale *bombardment* of Boston!

Washington decided to act as General Artemas Ward had done before him. Under cover of night, on 4 March he sent out 3,000 men to build a fort on Dorchester Heights, south of the city. Again Bostonians awoke to find a fortification where there had been an empty hill the evening before. Only this time the great guns of Ticonderoga were aimed at the city's heart. (Several are still there!)

General Howe, who had replaced Gage, mustered his troops for an attack by sea on Dorchester Heights. Luckily for the Americans a hurricane came up. The attack had to be put off for several days. The Americans used the delay to build another fort even closer to Boston, on Nook's Hill.

Was it the memory of the slaughter of Bunker Hill that made Howe afraid to attack? He decided not to go for the American position on Dorchester Heights, but to pull out from Boston entirely and make Nova Scotia, in Canada, his next base.

But this meant more than just transporting troops. Hundreds of Americans, loyal to the Crown, had been flocking into Boston for safety ever since Concord and Lexington. Howe could not leave them behind for Rebel vengeance.

They were packed into the British ships in the harbour, bound as they said 'For Hell, Hull, or Halifax'. They were the first thousand of 100,000 Americans who went into exile rather than live outside the British Empire. They called themselves Loyalists. The Rebels called them Tories and traitors, stole their goods, looted and confiscated the homes they left behind.

It was on St. Patrick's Day, 17 March 1776, that the British finally left Boston. They were unhindered by the Rebels. Howe warned Washington that he would set Boston afire if anyone tried to stop him from leaving with his army.

When the Americans pushed warily up to the deserted British lines, they found them quite empty, except for an occasional scarecrow draped in scarlet. About the neck of one hung a sign saying 'Welcome, Brother Jonathan'.

The next morning Washington rode into Boston. The siege was over! The city was in Rebel hands. But when and where would the British strike again?

While Washington was riding into a peaceful Boston, there was gunfire 600 miles to the north. In the summer of 1775, Congress had decided on a campaign against Canada. It had two good reasons. First, as long as Canada was in British hands New England and New York were in constant danger of invasion from the north. Secondly, they had the true zeal of converts.. In the enthusiasm of their rebellion they believed that the Canadians, too, must be ready to revolt against the Ministers of the King who, they believed, were taking their rights away.

An attack against Montreal was planned first. Sir Guy Carleton, commander of all British troops in Canada, had only 800 soldiers in the garrison in Montreal. The expedition was led by the energetic and experienced General Richard Montgomery. Ethan Allen, the New Hampshire man who had captured Fort Ticonderoga five months before, was sent ahead to persuade Canadians to enlist. Rashly he decided to attack Montreal on his own.

As his Green Mountain Boys advanced towards the

city, Carleton's regulars sallied out. All but forty of the Americans turned and ran. Some fled a mile before they were captured. Allen himself was taken and sent in chains for trial in England.

Allen's foolhardiness cost the Rebel cause much. Canadians who might have joined the Rebels, hesitated. The Loyalists remained convinced not only that it was right to remain loyal to Britain but that it was sensible. And the Indian tribes, who had not yet picked a side, chose the British as the winning one.

In spite of Allen's *fiasco*, Montgomery continued on the march. On 13 November he took Montreal and its entire garrison. Only one soldier managed to escape; Sir Guy Carleton, the commanding officer, got away in a canoe.

Quebec was the next goal. There was to be a two-pronged approach. One, under Montgomery, would come from Ticonderoga. Benedict Arnold would lead a *diversionary action*. His troops were to travel up through Maine. With Arnold was another

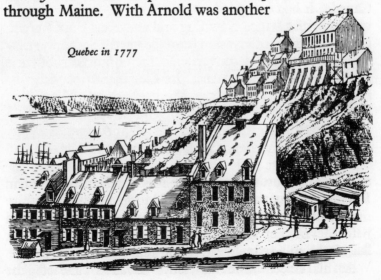

Quebec in 1777

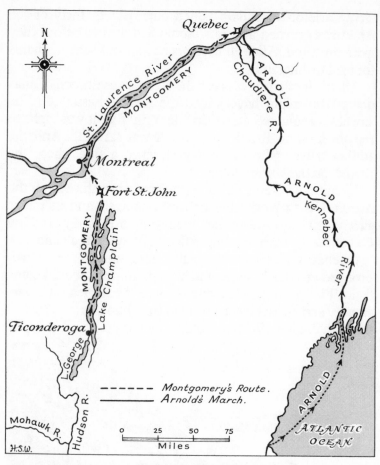

The invasion of Canada

soldier, afterwards famous. He was a rifleman expert in Indian warfare, the huge Daniel Morgan.

Arnold's force of 1,100 started out through the cold wilderness. They forded swift rivers and carried their big flat boats and sixty-five tons of supplies around rapids. When it rained the men's clothes froze 'a pane of glass thick'. The boats stove in and leaked. The food rotted. In their starvation, Arnold's men devoured shoe leather, soap, candles, even their pet dogs. Arnold had miscalculated the distance greatly. By 24 October his army had travelled seven days longer than he had expected, and was not even half-way to Quebec!

Early in December Montgomery's men and Arnold's 'famine-proof veterans', as they proudly called themselves, met outside Quebec's walls.

The two commanders faced a *dilemma*. They knew they had neither the time nor strength to besiege Quebec. They must attack the city head on—though that would cost many lives. They also knew they must do it soon. On 31 December the New Englanders' enlistments would run out. Without the encouragement of a victory they would take their guns and start home.

Both Arnold and Montgomery agreed that if they must assault Quebec it would be safest to do it under cover of a snowstorm.

On the very last day of the year a 'thick, small' snowstorm began. The Americans attacked. There was sharp street-fighting. Montgomery was killed and Arnold wounded. The invaders were driven back. Many escaped across the ice covering the Bay of St Charles, but about 400 were taken prisoner.

In spite of this defeat and his injuries, Arnold refused to give up. All winter he directed a siege of Quebec.

Smallpox broke out in his camp. He was injured again by a fall from his horse. In May Sir Guy Carleton drove the Americans back across the St Lawrence. The Rebels, under a new commander, Major-General John Sullivan, withdrew to the head of Lake Champlain and the safety of Ticonderoga.

A Quebec Loyalist wrote, 'Thus was the country freed

from a swarm of misguided people, led by *designing men*, enemies of the liberties of the country under the *specious* title of Assertors of American Rights.'

The thirteen rebellious colonies had to accept the fact that Canada wanted to remain in the Empire, and that across her borders, at any time, the British could launch an attack on them.

Independence Declared

During the first year few, if any, Rebels fought for freedom from the Empire. In March 1775, Benjamin Franklin told Lord Chatham that he had never heard any American, drunk or sober, hint that he wanted a permanent separation from England.

Even the battles of Concord and Lexington did not mean an open break. While Congress was creating an army and launching an invasion into Canada, it still hoped for *reconciliation*. As John Adams put it: 'Hold the sword in one hand and the olive branch in the other.'

This was the mood in which the Second Continental Congress in the Summer of 1775 sent 'The Olive Branch Petition' to King George.

Signed by forty-six delegates it was addressed to their 'Most Gracious Sovereign'. It said that the colonists earnestly wanted their 'former *harmony*' and a 'permanent reconciliation'. In the meantime it asked that the killing of 'Your Majesty's subjects' stop and the laws that distressed them be *repealed*.

King George refused to accept or read the petition. In August he proclaimed the Rebels 'wicked and desperate persons' and urged their countrymen to inform on their 'treasons and traitorous conspiracies'. In December he followed up this Proclamation with the *Prohibitory Acts*. They stated that the colonies were no longer under British protection, all American ports would be *blockaded*, and all American ships seized on the high seas.

The moderates in Congress were bitterly disappointed by the King's actions. As a Virginia delegate, Thomas Jefferson, wrote, 'It is an immense misfortune to the whole empire to have a king of such a *disposition* at such a time.' But the more fiery Rebels claimed that the king had now forced independence on them!

The colonies on the whole were now ready for the second document which would change the course of their history—a forty-seven-page *pamphlet* called COMMON SENSE.

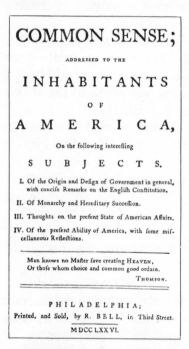

COMMON SENSE;

ADDRESSED TO THE

INHABITANTS

OF

AMERICA,

On the following interesting

SUBJECTS.

I. Of the Origin and Design of Government in general, with concise Remarks on the English Constitution.

II. Of Monarchy and Hereditary Succession.

III. Thoughts on the present State of American Affairs.

IV. Of the present Ability of America, with some miscellaneous Reflections.

Man knows no Master save creating HEAVEN,
Or those whom choice and common good ordain.
THOMSON.

PHILADELPHIA;
Printed, and Sold, by R. BELL, in Third Street.
MDCCLXXVI.

Title page of COMMON SENSE

COMMON SENSE was a highly emotional attack on the British Government, the King and the idea of royalty itself. Written by Tom Paine, a political *pamphleteer*, ex-corset maker and tax collector, its fiery message and rolling prose captured the colonial minds. It appeared in January 1776, and soon over 100,000 copies were circulating.

First, Tom Paine attacked the whole idea of having a king and then he went on to describe his ideal state (very unlike the one the United States has developed into) and ended with a dramatic last page. On a blank white sheet, in bold black letters appeared only seven words, 'THE FREE AND INDEPENDENT STATES OF AMERICA'. Cobblers, colonels, men, women, anyone who could read, read it. And as Washington said it worked a 'powerful change in the minds of many men'.

It pleaded with the American colonies to separate from the British Empire. Tom Paine wrote, 'Everything that is right or reasonable pleads for separation. The blood of the slain, the weeping voice of Nature cries "'Tis time to part".' And a North Carolina newspaper reported that COMMON SENSE 'made independents of the majority of the country'.

Six months later the rest of the country were made 'independents'. This was done by the Second Continental Congress. The document that announced it was the Declaration of Independence.

It was drafted by Thomas Jefferson, the brilliant, quiet, red-haired young Virginian with 'a happy talent for composition'.

When his fellow delegates asked him to write it, he was unwilling. But New Englander Adams felt that a Virginian should write the Declaration (as he had felt a Virginian should head the army).

Thomas Jefferson worked away in a second-storey parlour of the home of a German bricklayer in Philadelphia. He didn't want to work up people's feelings, as Tom Paine had done, but to place 'the common sense of the subject in terms so plain

Thomas Jefferson

Independence Hall in Philadelphia where the Declaration was signed

and firm as *to command assent*,' and to justify 'the independent stand we are compelled to take'.

His fellow congressmen made plenty of criticisms, suggestions and revisions, but the document was approved *unanimously*, and was signed by John Hancock on 4 July—by the other delegates in August and afterwards.

The Declaration is a successful attempt to justify the American Revolution. It uses ideas about laws and government that go far back into Greek, Roman and medieval times. It owes a great deal to the seventeenth-century English philosopher, John Locke. It also succeeds in being what Jefferson said he wanted it to be, 'an expression of the American mind'.

26

Here is the famous *preamble*:

When in the course of human events, it becomes necessary for one people to *dissolve* the political bands which have connected them with another and to assume among the powers of the earth the separate and equal *station* to which the laws of Nature and of Nature's God entitle them, a decent respect to the opinion of mankind requires that they should declare the causes which *impel* them to this separation.

We hold these truths to be *self-evident*, that all men are created equal, that they are endowed by their Creator with certain *inalienable* Rights, that among these are Life, Liberty and the pursuit of Happiness. That to secure these rights Governments are instituted among men *deriving* their just powers from the consent of the Governed.

The Declaration continues that whenever a government becomes 'destructive of these ends' the people have a right to alter or abolish it and to institute a new government.

It then lists twenty-seven *abuses* with which it accuses, not Parliament, not the royal Ministers, but King George III himself. It says that he refused assent to good laws, dissolved parliaments, *obstructed* justice, cut off their

Franklin's cartoon to make the colonies join together

27

trade, took away their charters, burnt their towns, deprived many of trial by jury. It goes through the list grimly and bitterly. Most of its charges were fair, some were not. The most important was 'imposing Taxes on us without our Consent'.

It was such a tax that caused the Boston Tea Party, the Intolerable Acts, Lexington and Concord, Bunker Hill. Because, as Lord Chatham had said almost two years before Independence was declared, 'No subject of England shall be taxed but by his own consent.'

This Declaration of Independence finally split the colonists clearly into two opposing parties, and each side had a name for itself and one for its enemies. Those who agreed with the Declaration called themselves Patriots, but to the opposite party they were Rebels. Those who remained loyal to the King and the British Government called themselves Loyalists, but to the other side they were Tories.

The Fight for New York City

While bells rang and bonfires blazed through the thirteen colonies to celebrate the adoption of the Declaration of Independence, in New York City, Washington was preparing for a British attack.

Washington had been in New York since 13 April 1776. Now in July, General Sir William Howe was sailing down from Halifax in Canada with an army of well-trained troops, while his brother, Admiral Lord Howe, was approaching with a large fleet. Both English and

Washington's New York Headquarters

New York Harbour in 1757

American commanders understood the strategic importance of New York. It lay between New England and the southern colonies: if one British army could drive up the Hudson River from New York City and join with another British army from Canada, between them they could cut New England off from the rest of the rebelling colonies. New York City could also be a base for an attack on Philadelphia, the home of the American Congress.

Because he had no experience as a general, Washington did not understand that in spite of the forts, cannons and barricades bristling through all the city, nothing could stop the British from taking it. New York City is on an island. It lies on a great harbour. Deep wide rivers rim two of its sides. A British fleet could capture it easily.

The British leaders had found it so hard to recruit Englishmen to fight against the Americans that King George had hired German soldiers. People in both Eng-

land and America were very angry about this. The Rebels called all these soldiers 'Hessians'.

Washington should have moved his army out of New York to the highlands of the Hudson River. From there he could have blocked Howe from marching north or from striking at Philadelphia. He made a big mistake. He tried to defend Brooklyn Heights, across New York Harbour, on Long Island.

On 22 August the Howe brothers landed a force on Long Island. General Howe did not attempt a head-on assault on Brooklyn Heights. He out-manœuvred Washington brilliantly, attacking the American flank after having found a way around by an unguarded road. The Americans were lured into the open and crushed. It was a very savage battle. The Hessians had been told that the Americans would kill all their prisoners, so they killed all the Americans they captured.

New York 1776

After his victory on Long Island, Sir William Howe did what he was going to do again and again during the Revolution. Nothing! Instead of following up his success he waited. He wasted several days.

While Howe waited, on the night of 29–30 August, Washington brought his army of 9,500 men safely across the East River from Brooklyn to New York. The army was rowed by a regiment of fishermen from Marblehead in Massachusetts. In heavy rain and thick fog, stealthily, the whole beaten army escaped out of Howe's trap.

Some historians believe that if the Declaration of Independence had not been adopted before the American defeat on Long Island, it might never have been adopted at all.

Both the Howes thought that the defeated Rebels must surely now sue for peace. (The Howes' chief wish was to make peace not war, anyway!) They wasted more time waiting to hear from Washington. Washington made no peace move.

He had decided at last that he must leave New York City. He was in the midst of moving his troops out when, on 15 September, Howe struck again. This time the British attacked the middle of Manhattan Island at a place called Kip's Bay. (It is now about 34th Street and the East River.)

First there was cannonading. Then boatloads of redcoats landed. (A Rebel private said they looked like a

Landing at Kip's Bay

'clover field in full bloom'.) As the British invaded the island, halting part-way across it, the Americans fled. Washington became so angry at his troops' cowardice, he lost all self-control. Cursing, he hit about him with his riding-crop. In the daze that followed this outburst of temper he was almost captured.

It seemed as though the several thousand American soldiers caught in New York City south of Kip's Bay must be captured. But a Mrs Robert Murray (a middle-aged mother of twelve, not the young beauty of American legend) invited Sir William into her house for wine and cake. While British soldiers waited outside in the broiling sun, the officers rested in Mrs Murray's shady parlour. They rested just ten minutes too long to prevent the last Americans under General Israel Putnam from escaping!

Washington had brought his whole army safely out of Manhattan. Two days later a great fire broke out in the city he had given up so unwillingly. A quarter of the city was burnt. The morning after the fire there was a sudden hanging. A Rebel captain, a schoolmaster from New Haven, Connecticut, named Nathan Hale, had volunteered to slip into the city for information. As he was leaving with his information, he was identified and captured. A contemporary newspaper reported that Hale, on suspicion of being a spy (and of starting the fire), was 'taken up and dragged without ceremony to the execution post and hung up'. His words, 'I only regret I have but one life to lose for my country,' are among the most stirring in American history.

For almost a month, Howe left Washington alone on rocky Harlem Heights. The American army seemed about to collapse. There were hundreds of desertions. Washington lacked competent officers. He said his surgeons, for instance, 'were very great rascals'. General Henry Knox, who had brought the cannon from Ticonderoga to Boston, described the army outside of New York as a 'receptacle for ragamuffins'.

While Washington worked, watched and worried, Howe lagged. Finally, on 28 October 1776, he met and beat Washington once more, yet again he failed to follow up his victory.

Howe moved next against the two Hudson River strongholds north of New York, Fort Washington and Fort Lee. On the night of 16 November, at Fort Washington, the Americans lost 2,800 men, 146 cannon and masses of ammunition. Three days later, in a dawn attack, Fort Lee, on the opposite side of the Hudson, was seized by Howe. As one British officer wrote: 'The rebels fled like scared rabbits . . . they left some poor pork, a few greasy proclamations, and some of that scoundrel COMMON SENSE man's letters which we can read at our leisure now that we have got one of the *impregnable* redoubts of Mr Washington *to quarter* in.' (New York City was to be British-held until 1783!)

Washington and his army—now down to 3,000—were on the run. Dodging through New Jersey, keeping one day's march away from the British, the Rebels seemed, as one redcoat put it, to be playing Bo Peep. Washington knew how desperate his plight was. But he told one of his aides, 'My neck does not feel as if it were made for a halter,' and gave no sign of surrendering.

By now many of Washington's critics and even his friends began to doubt that he could win the war. He himself, when he had accepted his generalship had said, 'I do not think myself equal to the command.' Since he had arrived in New York from Boston in April, Washington had lost skirmishes and battles, forts and cities. Five thousand of his men were prisoners. His army had shrunk from 20,000 to 3,000.

One of his generals, Charles Lee, complained about Washington's failures. He was just finishing a letter in which he said, 'A certain great man is damnably *deficient*' when he was captured—in dressing-gown and slippers—by a detachment of British dragoons! One of Lee's staff who had listened to his complaining thought it was a trick to get over to the British. 'What a damn sneaking way of being kidnapped!' he cried. But Washington, who depended heavily on General Lee, wrote to Congress, 'Our cause has received a severe blow.'

December 1776 was half-way over. Washington knew that unless he heartened his soldiers with a victory most of them would go home when their enlistments ran out on the thirty-first. He determined to try for such a victory.

Washington's plan included a Christmas night crossing of the ice-choked Delaware River, and an attack on the town of Trenton, New Jersey, which was held by the Hessian troops.

The regiment of blue-jacketed fishermen from Marblehead who had rowed the American Army to safety after the defeat on Long Island was again at the oars. Once across the Delaware River, despite raw cold and wild snowstorms, the troops, as General Knox wrote his wife, 'marched with the most profound silence and good order'.

The Hessian Colonel, Johannes Rall, and his men had been over-celebrating Christmas with rum and wine. The American attack roused their sentries from drunken sleep. Rall was slain. In forty-five minutes almost 1,000 prisoners were taken. There were only five American casualties.

After the battle, the Rebels marched back nine freezing miles in the storm and re-crossed the Delaware. When their boat bottoms became caked with ice, both captors and prisoners jumped up and down, their pigtails flapping, until the ice fell off.

New Jersey and Pennsylvania

On the last day of the year, Washington urged his soldiers to re-enlist and the drum beat for volunteers. Not a man stepped forward. Washington said, 'If you will consent to stay only one month longer, you will render that service to the cause of liberty and your country which probably you never can do under any other circumstances.' When the drums beat again, his whole gaunt, tattered army answered his appeal.

The victory at Trenton made the British call in another general. Lord Cornwallis arrived at Trenton on the night of 2 January and was advised to attack the Americans immediately. He said he could 'just as well bag the fox next morning'. His quartermaster said: 'My Lord, if you trust these people tonight, you will see nothing of them in the morning.' The quartermaster was right. Knowing the British outnumbered him, Washington muffled his cannon wheels and, leaving his camp-fires burning, spirited his army away to Princeton.

In a short, fierce battle with some British troops at Princeton, the Redcoats began to run. Washington spurred after them shouting: 'It's a fine fox chase, my boys!' But he could not hold the town, for his men were weary and Cornwallis was near. Finally he withdrew his army to a mountain plateau in New Jersey where he could watch British movements in New York and guard the road between New England and Philadelphia.

His army, half-naked, worn out and stricken with small-pox, waited there for spring. Howe, in the comfort of New York, let them alone.

The Road to Saratoga

'John Burgoyne *wagers* Charles Fox one pony [50 guineas] that he will be home victorious from America by Christmas Day, 1777.' So runs the first wager in an eighteenth-century betting-book in Brooks's Club in London.

Dashing General John Burgoyne had a plan to win the war against the Rebels. He described it in a paper he presented to King George III. The paper was called

General John Burgoyne

39

'Thoughts for Conducting the War from the Side of Canada'. The King and his ministers approved, so on 6 May 1777, Burgoyne arrived in Quebec, Canada, ready to put his plan into action.

It consisted of a three-pronged attack. One army (under Burgoyne himself) was to come down the Hudson from Canada to Albany, a town at the centre of the state, now

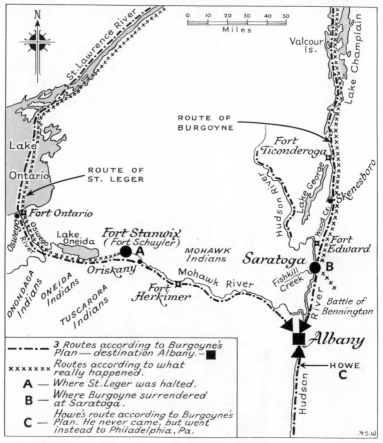

Burgoyne's Plan and What Happened

General Sir William Howe

the capital of the State of New York. The second army,
under Barry St Leger, was to cross the Mohawk Valley
from Oswego and meet Burgoyne at Albany. The third
army (under General Howe) was to come up the Hudson
River from New York City to Albany. When the three
armies met, the New England colonies would be cut off
from the rest of the nation.

On paper the plan seemed good. Its success, however,
depended on two essentials that were not there. Clear
commands must come from London *co-ordinating* Howe's
and Burgoyne's moves. Howe and Burgoyne must work
together and keep in touch with each other. But neither

of these things happened. King George was badly served by his ministers, especially by Lord George Germain, Head of the Colonial Office, and in charge of the general plan of the war. It was partly his fault that the Burgoyne plan failed. Some historians say that he did not send the proper orders to America because he was in a hurry to start his holiday. Others say he sent contradictory orders to Burgoyne and Howe.

First, Germain approved Burgoyne's plan but shortly afterwards he approved a different plan of General Howe's. Howe wanted to move against Philadelphia instead of marching north to Albany. Since Germain had no understanding of the difficulties of wilderness warfare in America, he may have thought Howe could first take Philadelphia and then go to Burgoyne's help in the north before winter came.

But Burgoyne was told nothing of Howe's new plan. When, in June 1777, he started down the Great Lakes towards Albany, he believed that Howe was on his way to meet him.

Ticonderoga was easily captured by Burgoyne—a great blow to the Rebels, who then retreated to Fort Edward with Burgoyne following close behind. In his efforts to catch up with the Rebels, Burgoyne made his first serious mistake. A Loyalist adviser, Philip Skene, persuaded him to take his army by land instead of water. (Skene had a vast property in the area. He wanted the British Army to build a road through it.)

Burgoyne plunged into the swampy, pathless forests. The route was made harder because Rebels felled giant pines to block the path, destroyed bridges and scattered boulders in his way. Soon Burgoyne's army was completely bogged down. With its forty-two pieces of heavy artillery it could advance only a mile a day. Supplies were running out, the mosquitoes and flies were a black plague.

The Rebel commander, General Philip Schuyler, had crippled Burgoyne's advance but his forces were not strong. Local volunteers were not keen to join up. Then a crime by two of Burgoyne's Red Indians turned the local farmers over to the Rebel side. The Indians killed and scalped a young girl engaged to a Tory officer. When one of them returned to the British camp with Jane McCrea's scalp in his belt, Burgoyne did not punish him. He feared the other Indians would resent it and desert if he did. This, of course, angered everyone. 'Remember Jane McCrea' became a frontier war-cry. Farmers seized their muskets and set out to join Schuyler.

While Burgoyne's ponderous army was lumbering south to Albany, Colonel Barry St Leger was leading the 'second prong of the attack' up the Mohawk Valley. When he reached a small log fort on the Mohawk River, Fort Stanwix (where the city of Rome, N.Y., is now) he demanded its surrender. But the valley men inside the fort ran up no white flag. Instead they raised a banner the British had never seen before. It had thirteen red and white stripes and a circle of thirteen white stars on a dark blue field. It was the new American flag. It had been designed by George Washington and a fashionable Philadelphia dressmaker, Betsy Ross.

The women inside Fort Stanwix had read a description of the newly-designed flag in a newspaper. They made this one from a red petticoat, a white shirt and the blue coat of a British officer. Over the little frontier fort of Fort Stanwix, the Star Spangled Banner was flown for the first time in battle. St Leger surrounded Fort Stanwix with his regulars and war-whooping Indians and laid siege to it. The fort refused to give in. An old general and Dutch

43

farmer, Nicholas Herkimer, who lived in a big red house on the Mohawk River, set out with 800 volunteers to break the siege. He was ambushed near a ravine in Oriskany. His horse was shot from under him. His leg was shattered. Although mortally wounded, propped up against a tree trunk, he directed the battle. The Mohawk Valley militia formed a circle around him in the woods, and with knife and musket, pistol and tomahawk, drove the Indians off.

Two weeks later General Benedict Arnold (the Connecticut apothecary who had led the campaign into Canada) arrived to help Fort Stanwix. He had only 950 soldiers, none of them from the district around, so he decided to trick St Leger into thinking he was far stronger than he was. Arnold persuaded Hon Yost, a feeble-minded boy, to go into St Leger's camp with news that a great Rebel army was coming. (They shot bullet-holes through Hon Yost's jacket to support the story.)

When Hon ran into St Leger's camp and the Indians

White settlement in the Mohawk Valley

asked how many Americans were coming, he babbled and pointed to the leaves on the trees. Three Indians, secretly friendly to the Rebels, followed with even more frightening stories of the vast army approaching.

An Indian chief approached St Leger. He said: 'When we marched down you told us there would be no fighting for us Indians. We might go down and smoke our pipes,

The first American flag

A British camp

but now a number of our warriors have been killed and you mean to sacrifice us.' Despite St Leger's protests, the chief departed with 800 men. St Leger had to give up the siege of Fort Stanwix.

In the meantime, Burgoyne was getting desperately short of food. The Americans had destroyed everything that could feed his army. All corn had been laid waste, all cattle driven off. On 20 August Burgoyne wrote a bitter letter to Lord George Germain. He complained that the American Loyalists did not help him enough. He grumbled because he could not get in touch with Howe. His messengers, he wrote, had been caught by the Rebels and hanged. He ended gloomily: 'I little foresaw I was to be left to pursue my way through such a tract of country without any co-operation from New York.'

By September, Burgoyne knew that Howe was definitely on his way to Philadelphia instead of coming to meet him. He could expect no help from him. Burgoyne faced a cruel choice. Should he attack on his own and reach Albany before winter? Should he retreat to the safety of Ticonderoga? Burgoyne, always a gambler, decided to attack.

On 13 and 14 September he crossed to the west bank of the Hudson River and prepared to move against the Rebel posts. His spy system was poor. His Indians were deserting. There were 7,000 Americans commanded by Horatio Gates (who had replaced Schuyler) against Burgoyne's 6,000 soldiers. Militia had swarmed in from all over New England and New York. General Benedict Arnold was back. Washington had sent up Colonel Daniel Morgan and his *sharpshooters*. Every day the American army grew.

Under the guidance of the brilliant Polish engineer, Thaddeus Kosciusko, the Americans had built strong defences. Burgoyne attacked head-on. Morgan's rifles repulsed him. Three weeks later there was another unsuccessful *assault* by Burgoyne. He had now lost 1,200 men. As he tried to retreat to Saratoga, he was followed by an army three times the size of his, for more militia kept joining the American side. Burgoyne's food was running out.

On 7 October 1777, the two armies met and Burgoyne was thrown back. Benedict Arnold, who had been confined to his tent after a dispute with General Gates, rushed out, leapt on a borrowed horse, and led the charge. Burgoyne's men were driven back, suffering losses five times the Americans'. Arnold was shot in the same leg that had been injured at Quebec.

Two days later Burgoyne retreated to Saratoga. Swarming like birds of prey, American militia pushed behind him, cutting off his escape. He despaired of help from Clinton. On 17 October Burgoyne surrendered. Clinton, coming to help him, heard the bad news and quickly returned to New York.

But where was General Howe during the summer of 1777, when Burgoyne thought he was coming north to help him? He was planning a campaign to take Philadelphia, 'the Rebel capital'. Washington tried to stop him but finally Howe tricked him into marching north—out of the way. At last the road to Philadelphia was clear of Americans! Unhindered, Howe marched into Philadelphia on 26 September. But once there, he did very little else. He had captured the city but failed to destroy Washington's army. He had left Burgoyne alone to lose seven generals, 300 officers and over 5,000 men at Saratoga. Howe could win battles—he never lost one to Washington—but he never managed to get real results from his victories.

British cartoon showing General Howe doing nothing

Saratoga is one of the decisive battles of history. After it, the British gave up hope of a successful invasion of the colonies from Canada. More important, France, who had been helping America secretly, now came openly to her aid.

On 6 February 1778, France recognized the new republic. She signed a treaty promising full military support to the United States. She declared war on England. Spain and Holland followed her example a year later.

When the King's ministers in London heard about Burgoyne's surrender, Lord North presented the *Conciliatory Proposals* to Parliament. Almost every American grievance was removed—even Parliament's claim to the right to tax the colonies. Lord North said that there was so much affection left in the colonies for England, 'that barely to enter on the discussion was half the business.'

It was not easy for Lord North to persuade Parliament to agree to the Conciliatory Proposals. Many members thought their *corrupt* and incompetent rulers, having lost them an army at Saratoga and dragged them into a World War, were panicking instead of facing up to danger.

Lord Chatham, America's great champion, though desperately ill, dragged himself to Parliament and gave a stirring speech. He first attacked the *dismemberment* 'of this ancient and noble monarchy'. He attacked the Tory government for using German mercenaries against American colonials. He said, 'My lords, if I were an American, as I am an Englishman, while a foreign troop was landed in my country I never would lay down my arms—never, never, never.' When he tried to speak again he collapsed and was carried out, to die a month later.

A few months earlier America might have accepted North's offer but now she refused. The victory at Saratoga and the French Treaty made the change. America now had a powerful ally and a European fleet to help her. England was suddenly caught in another World War in which her American colonial campaigns were only a small part. That was what that gunfire at Lexington had brought England to—World War.

British cartoon: the horse America throwing his master

France Comes In

France's entry into the war in February 1778, was the result of much plotting by American diplomats whom Congress had sent to Paris. The aim of the Americans in Europe was to stir up European powers against England, and to get the help of a foreign navy.

Early in the war, Congress set up two committees for this purpose. The first, the Secret Committee, under a merchant, Robert Morris, organized the already widespread smuggling of European goods to America. The second, the Committee of Secret Correspondence, hired spies and tried to find foreign allies. This second Committee was headed by Benjamin Franklin, a plain, seventy-year-old scholar, writer and scientist. He was used to Europe; for eighteen years he had been a colonial agent in London.

After the defeat of Long Island and the retreat through New Jersey, the French began to doubt if America could win. Shrewd old Franklin argued with the Comte de Vergennes, France's foreign minister. He told Vergennes that when France helped America, she was just getting her revenge for the beating in the Seven Years War. He reminded Vergennes that if America lost the Revolution and had to return to the British Empire the Empire would be stronger than before. Vergennes saw Franklin's point.

Besides sending money and supplies, Europe helped the Americans through experienced army officers who volunteered to fight for the Rebel side. Some were self-seeking

Benjamin Franklin

fortune-hunters; many did a great work for America. The
French Louis du Portail and Polish Thaddeus Kosciusko
were clever engineers. Casimir Pulaski, another Pole,
organized the first American cavalry regiment. Baron
Wilhelm von Steuben reorganized and trained the whole
army during the winter of Valley Forge. Most famous and
loved of all was the young Frenchman, the Marquis de
Lafayette. He became a major-general in the American
army by the age of twenty-one but never took a penny for
his services.

When, on 1 December 1777, news of the victory of
Saratoga finally reached Paris, the French cheered in
their streets and squares 'as if it had been a victory of
their own troops over their own enemies'. Vergennes now

realized that England would probably try to make peace with her colonies. She might even offer them independence. He wrote to the French ambassador in Madrid, 'The power that first recognizes the independence of the Americans will be the one to gather all the fruits of the war.' The next day the Crown Council of France agreed to conclude the *alliance* and Vergennes sent Franklin word that France would enter the war openly on the American side.

Although the American–French Treaty was signed in February 1778, it was May before the news could reach America. During the long cold months, Washington's army shivered and starved in their winter camp in Valley Forge. Many of the troops had no shoes, breeches, stockings or blankets. Since the camp had to be fortified before huts could be built, the men froze in tattered tents well into January. As Washington wrote to Congress, they 'occupy a cold, bleak hill and sleep under frost and snow'. Since soap and water were as scarce as food and clothes, their sores festered and bodies itched.

Much of this tragic suffering was unnecessary. Food shortages were due to mismanagement and inefficiency. There was grain in the Pennsylvania countryside, but no wagons to haul it into camp; there was meat, but no salt to keep it from rotting. Congress, driven out of Philadelphia by Howe, was torn with disagreements. But, while Congressmen bickered and blundered, the men at Valley Forge went barefoot in the snow and supped 'as usual on a leg of nothing and no turnips'. One of the reasons for this mismanagement was the weakness of the government. In November 1777 the thirteen states had signed an agreement among themselves called 'The Articles of Confederation and Perpetual Union'. This agreement was a 'league of friendship' and little more. It was fatally weak because

THIRTY SIX·SHILLINGS.

Issued in defence of American Liberty.

Ense petit placidam sub Libertate. Quietem

MAGNA CHARTA

Decm.̄ 7. 1775.

Paper money issued by Congress, engraved by Paul Revere

it did not give Congress power to enforce laws over the thirteen states or to get things done. Worst of all, Congress could not levy taxes. It had no way of raising money to run the government well. So it could never feed, clothe or pay the men in the army properly. That is why there was so much grumbling, suffering and even mutiny in the army as the war went on.

But Washington's army survived the winter. Indeed, they marched out of Valley Forge far better soldiers than they had marched in. This was because a German volunteer, Wilhelm von Steuben, had been training them. He was a bald, big-nosed Prussian officer who had been fifteen years out of work when Benjamin Franklin met him in Paris and sent him to Washington. He set up drill teams, reorganized the army, wrote a handbook of arms. He spoke no English and when his soldiers could not understand his commands, he begged his interpreters to 'come and swear for me in English'.

How well Von Steuben understood American soldiers is shown in a letter to a friend in Europe: 'In the first place the genius of this nation is not in the least to be compared with that of Prussians, Austrians and French. You say to your soldier "Do this," and he does it, but I am obliged to say "This is the reason why you ought to do that" and then he does it.'

54

Washington made a second important appointment in Valley Forge. In March 1778, Nathanael Greene became *Quartermaster*-General. Greene was a soldierly, industrious, intelligent, husky man, with a limp. His efficiency meant that starving soldiers now ate, and naked ones were clothed.

With May came the news of the French treaty. Washington said, 'I believe no event was ever received with more heartfelt joy,' and prepared for his summer campaign.

In March 1778 Howe, who had wintered comfortably in Philadelphia, heard that Sir Henry Clinton was replacing him as General. Howe was given a great farewell party in Philadelphia. It was called a Mischianza and was attended by Tory ladies in 'dazzling Turkish costumes'. There was a mock tournament, a band, fireworks and dancing until four in the morning.

On his arrival in Philadelphia, Clinton got orders to abandon the city, since it could not be held against the expected French fleets. He planned to retreat to New York by land, fearing that if he went by sea the French might attack him. In June 1778, the long files of British soldiers started out from Philadelphia. Heavily laden, marching in the broiling sun, they were a tempting target for Washington. Should he harass and snipe at them or try a full attack?

General Lee (the officer who had been captured by the British in dressing-gown and slippers) was now back with Washington after a winter as a prisoner in New York. He had only lately been exchanged and did not realize what Von Steuben's training had done for the army at Valley Forge. Washington sent Lee to attack the British near Monmouth. Lee did not attack as he had been ordered because he thought Clinton's troops were too

General Charles Lee

strong. His men began to retreat, then to run. Washington
sent a messenger to ask why. When he returned, Washington galloped forward, angrily asking why Lee had not
attacked. 'Sir, these troops are not able to meet British
Grenadiers!' 'Sir, they are able and by God they will!'
Washington thundered. A Virginia general said later of
Washington: 'Sir, he swore on that day till the leaves
shook on the trees. Sir, on that ever memorable day, he
swore like an angel from heaven.'

Washington stopped the retreat, rallied the men, and
there was a sharp battle. That night Washington slept on
the field. He planned to continue the battle next day. But
while he slept, Clinton and his whole army slipped away
from Monmouth and made it in safety to New York City.

Sea Battles and Indian Warfare

From that March day, back in 1776, when Washington watched General Howe sail safely away from Boston, and then again safely into New York Harbour in July 1776, he longed for the help of a European navy. Now that France had come into the war on the American side, and a French fleet was on its way across the Atlantic, Washington had high hopes of ending the war. He believed that if an American army and French fleet together launched an attack against the British, victory could be had.

Great Britain now hoped to end the war too—by *conciliation*. In June 1778, the Earl of Carlisle arrived in Philadelphia with peace offers from Parliament granting almost everything the colonists had demanded at the start of the war. There would be no standing army in the colonies. There would be no changes in colonial charters unless America wanted them. Either Americans could send representatives to Parliament, or if preferred, Congress would be recognized as an American Parliament. Most important, there would be 'no taxation without representation'.

The, President of Congress, Henry Laurens, said: 'If all the fine things now offered had been offered some time ago' there is no doubt they would have been accepted. But now, 'they seem to mistake our understanding as once they did our *resolution*'. Even Carlisle himself soon saw how useless his efforts were. 'The leaders on the enemy's side are too powerful,' he wrote his wife, 'the common people hate us in their hearts.'

Less than a month after Congress rejected the Carlisle offer, the French fleet arrived outside of New York Harbour. Washington was overjoyed. The French had three times the British firing power. They could sail into the Harbour and destroy the British fleet lying at anchor there. But the French Admiral, Charles d'Estaing, was afraid that his big ships would run aground on the sand bar that blocked the mouth of the Harbour. He refused to try to cross it.

When, after ten days of discussion, Washington saw that the French would not attack the British fleet at New York he persuaded d'Estaing to move against the second most important British-held seaport in America—Newport, in Rhode Island. D'Estaing began the siege, but gave it up after a hurricane, known as the 'Great French Storm', had damaged his ships. Angry at American criticism, he sailed away to the West Indies. During these two unsuccessful attempts at a joint American land and French sea action against the British, Washington had withdrawn to White Plains near New York. He was in the same position he had held in 1776 before his retreat across New Jersey. He was to spend the rest of the war in this district, refusing to risk his army and waiting for another chance for a decisive blow in co-operation with a French fleet.

The most effective sea weapons the Americans had against the British were privateers, or privately owned sea raiders. During the Revolution 2,000 American raiders destroyed $18,000,000 worth of British ships and cargoes. British merchants lost so much that many became eager for the war's end. The most famous American privateer was a Scottish-born sea captain, John Paul Jones. During the war he sailed up and down the Channel attacking

merchant ships and sea-
ports and then returning
to French or Dutch
harbours for safety.

Jones's most famous
victory took place in the
North Sea. He commanded
the *Bonhomme Richard*, an
ancient Indiaman supplied
by the French. (Its name
was a French translation of
Poor Richard, Benjamin
Franklin's pen name.)

The *Bonhomme Richard*,
and three small ships with
her, attacked a British
convoy which was being
escorted by two British
men-o'-war, the *Serapis*
and *Countess of Scar-*

Captain John Paul Jones

borough. The convoy escaped. Jones manœuvred his ship
close to the *Serapis* and lashed the two ships together. All
night they fought; at times both were in flames. When the
Bonhomme Richard seemed to be sinking and the British
captain summoned Jones to surrender, Jones answered:
'I have not yet begun to fight!' At dawn the *Serapis'*
powder magazine blew up. Her guns were wrecked and
everyone behind the mainmast killed. Her captain surrendered and 'the two captains now withdrew into the
cabin and there drank a glass or two of wine together'.
Two days later, the war-torn *Bonhomme Richard* sank in
the North Sea.

Just as American privateers harried British shipping
constantly all through the Revolution, so Indian braves

harried the American frontier settlements. In those days the western frontier stretched in a long curve from Maine southward to Georgia. Over it the Indian menace hung 'like a *scythe* of death'.

The Indians bitterly resented how the Americans kept moving westwards, clearing the ground and building cabins and destroying ancient Indian hunting grounds. So most Indians were allies of the British during the Revolu-

Lonely frontier log cabin

tion, attacking and destroying lonely frontier homes and the families of the Americans. People in both England and America condemned the use of Indians in the war. But, although the British used the Indians much more than the Americans, they were not the first to do it. There were Indians among the Minute Men in the battle of Lexington. In 1775 Congress told its Indian Commissioners to try to keep the Indians neutral or else enlist them on the American side. But, because the British gave more in the way of gifts and promises and because at first it looked as if

Cherokee Indian warrior

the British would win the war, the Indian chieftains sided with the British and their Tory allies.

Indians marched with Burgoyne to Saratoga. (Their murder of Jane McCrea did much to turn neutral farmers into Rebels.) Indians were with St Leger during the siege of Fort Stanwix—and left him after Oriskany. The British Army never did—or perhaps could—use Indians very sensibly. In the long run Indians probably did more harm than good to the British side. Their sneak raids, scalpings and burnings turned many frontiersmen against the British and Tories.

One of the most dramatic campaigns against the Indians was led by a tall, young, red-haired surveyor and

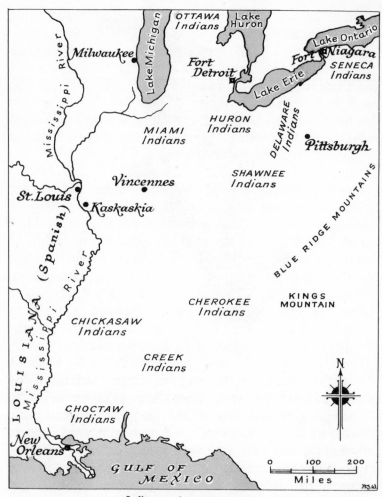

Indians on the western frontier

experienced fighter, George Rogers Clark. It was against the southern Indian tribes. The British supply base for these Indians was Fort Detroit, commanded by Colonel Henry Hamilton. (His nickname was 'The Hair Buyer' because he was supposed to have offered rewards for American scalps.)

In June 1778 Clark organized a band of 175 Virginia frontiersmen. He floated them down the Ohio River and led them on a 120-mile march to French-held Kaskaskia, now in the State of Illinois. When the French settlers heard about the American–French treaty they agreed to help Clark. He captured several French towns, including Vincennes in present-day Indiana.

In December, in a swirling snowstorm, Hamilton re-took Vincennes. Clark said 'an enemy could not suppose we should be so mad as to attempt to march eighty leagues through a drowned country in the depth of winter'. They would be off their guard and 'not think it worthwhile to keep out spies'. So he marched his 170 men through flooded stretches of icy water, sometimes shoulder-deep When he finally recaptured Vincennes, Clark cold-bloodedly executed some Indian captives while their tribesmen looked on—to convince the tribesmen that the British could not protect them. He then claimed territory more than half the size of all thirteen colonies, for Virginia.

Another much larger campaign was organized by Congress in 1779 against one of the most powerful Indian tribes—the Six Nations of the Iroquois. General John Sullivan led the campaign. Sullivan's expedition was in revenge for the Tory and Indian raids.

In July 1778, Tory Colonel John Butler, with 500 Senecas, had attacked Wyoming Valley in Pennsylvania, destroying a thousand homes. In September, Indians wiped out a Mohawk Valley village. Then in November Tories and Indians attacked Cherry Valley, a village about fifty miles west of Albany, N.Y.

Sullivan was sent to stop such raids. Washington ordered him: the country of the Six Nations must not be

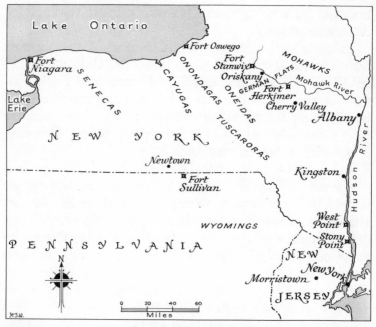

Iroquois Indian Country

'merely overrun but destroyed'. He led 5,000 men through
400 miles of wilderness, aiming to capture Fort Niagara—
the main British supply base for the Iroquois.

On 29 August 1779, in Newtown, near Elmira, N.Y.,
Sullivan beat an army of Indians and Tories. He burnt
more than forty Indian towns, laid hundreds of acres of
grain and orchards to waste. Hundreds of Iroquois died
of disease and starvation the next winter. He could not,
however, reach Fort Niagara, and so failed to cut off the
Iroquois war-making power at its source. In 1780, the
Iroquois survivors were back on the warpath. Blazing with
revenge, they looted and killed more savagely than before.

The sprawling frontier still lived in terror of Indian
raids.

The Sword in the South

The Treaty with France brought the French into open war against England in February 1778. A year later Spain and Holland also entered the war on the American side. With three European powers and America united against her, England began to show the stout heart that has carried her through world wars ever since. She started an attack in the southern states. She used her Loyalist Volunteers more successfully.

In November 1778 Clinton sent 3,500 men under Lieutenant-Colonel Archibald Campbell down to attack the busy port city of Savannah, Georgia. General Augustine Prevost came up from Florida to join him. At first the Rebels, under General Robert Howe, tried to beat off the attack. Then an old Negro led Campbell's men through the wooded swamps until they were behind Howe. Assaulted on both sides, the Americans panicked and fled—many were drowned in the swamps. The American losses were eighty-three dead, 453 captured. Three British were killed and ten wounded. After this capture of Savannah, the British once more ruled in Georgia.

The following September, the French fleet under Admiral d'Estaing appeared off the Georgia coast. The combined American and French forces were 5,000 against 3,200 British. On 4 October 1779, French and American batteries began shelling Savannah. The bombardment was so fierce that of 450 homes there was hardly one that 'had not been shot through'. But d'Estaing was afraid of what

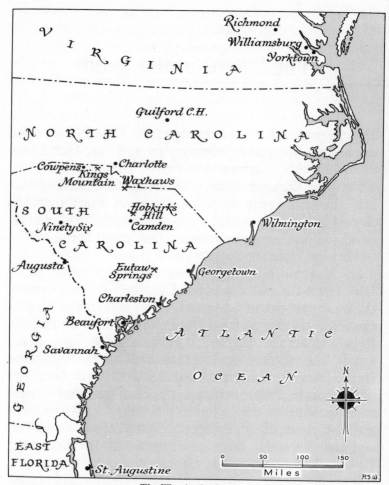

The War in the South

autumn storms could do to his fleet. In spite of protests, he insisted on a head-on dawn attack on Savannah. It was a disaster. It was the battle of Bunker Hill the other way round, with the French and Americans taking the losses. The allies lost more than 800, the British only 150.

66

D'Estaing refused to carry on the siege and sailed away. Another attempt at a joint American land and French sea action had failed, leaving the Americans very bitter.

The Americans' failure to capture Savannah was followed in the spring by a greater blow to the Rebel cause— the loss of the city of Charleston, South Carolina.

Sir Henry Clinton attacked Charleston by land, with a far larger army than that defending it. The city was soon surrounded. The one escape route was cut off by two British officers, Lieutenant-Colonel Banastre Tarleton and Major Patrick Ferguson, with their Tory regiments. The siege lasted a month. Each day the British moved nearer the city. On 9 May 1780, the British offered peace terms. The Americans answered with a bombardment. 'Shells like *meteors* crossed each other, cannon balls whizzing, shells hissing, ammunition chests blowing up.'

After this last defiance, as the American Colonel William Moultrie wrote later in his memoirs, we 'began to cool, and we cooled gradually, and on the 11 May we *capitulated* and on the morning of the twelfth we marched out'.

A British officer described the surrender of Charleston thus: 'The General limped out at the head of the most ragged *rabble* I ever beheld. . . . They laid down their arms. . . . The militia began to creep out of their holes the next day.' The British took 5,000 prisoners and masses of supplies. It was the greatest American disaster of the war.

Colonel Moultrie also recalled that an English captain said to him, 'Sir, you have made a gallant defence, but you have a great many rascals among you who came out every night and gave us information of what was passing in your garrison.'

Not only was Charleston lost but 350 Virginians who had been marching to its rescue were attacked by Tarleton, near Waxhaws Creek, in South Carolina. Tarleton claimed

Colonel Banastre Tarleton

afterwards that the Rebels seemed about to fire on his white flag of truce. In any case, he permitted his soldiers to massacre every surrendering American. It was 'a bloody day, that wanted only the war-dance and roasting-fire to have it placed first in the records of torture and death in the West'. The massacre of Waxhaws inspired the Rebel war-cry 'Tarleton's Quarter! Tarleton's Quarter!' and was used as an excuse for much future Rebel cruelty.

South Carolina was in British hands. So was Georgia. Clinton, satisfied, returned to New York City, leaving Lord Cornwallis to carry on the campaign to subdue the south with 8,000 soldiers. Cornwallis set up bases along the coast at Savannah, Beaufort, Charleston and Georgetown.

But American *guerrillas* undercut Cornwallis's communications, struck at his outposts and attacked his Tories. The Revolution in the south became a bitter civil war—much of its cruelty caused by revenge for the massacre at Waxhaws. Families were torn apart. Friends and neighbours became savage enemies and the whole country sprang into 'an absolute state of rebellion'.

Congress, without consulting Washington, named

Horatio Gates, General in the south. Stupidly, he began a march through wilderness swampland, swarming with Tories. Although his men were sick, tired and hungry, on 15 August he ordered a night march, boasting: 'I will breakfast tomorrow with Lord Cornwallis at my table'—as a prisoner, of course.

Cornwallis had ordered a night march too. The two armies were startled to meet half-way, in a pine forest, at about two in the morning. Cornwallis arranged his battle line carefully to await the dawn. Gates, just as the fight was starting, suddenly tried to shift his exhausted, untrained militia. Confusion resulted. The British Light Infantry took advantage of it and charged. Only a handful of regular Rebel soldiers stood their ground. Cornwallis, seeing that no cavalry opposed him, pushed his dragoons on and his infantry smashed ahead with fixed bayonets. The Rebel militia threw down their arms and ran.

General Gates, on an excellent horse, ran faster than anyone else. He did not stop running until he reached Charlotte, North Carolina, sixty miles from the battle. A month later a sarcastic advertisement appeared in a New York City newspaper. It began:

REWARD

Strayed, lost or stolen . . . on the 17 August last, near Camden, in the State of South Carolina, a whole ARMY consisting of horse, foot and dragoons, to the amount of near TEN THOUSAND. . . .

Alexander Hamilton, George Washington's secretary (later to be the first American Secretary of the Treasury), wrote even more scornfully of Gates's cowardice, 'Was there ever an instance of a general running away as Gates has done from his whole army? . . . One hundred and eighty miles in three days and a half. It does admirable credit to the activity of a man at his time of life. But it disgraces the general and the soldier.'

Hunger and Treachery

The war in the Northern States seemed to stand still. Two winters and a summer passed without any great battle.

In the spring of 1779 Sir Henry Clinton received orders from London: 'Bring Mr Washington to a decisive and general action' (that is, beat him in one big battle). But Clinton found it hard to do this, for Washington was determined not to risk his whole army in one battle, unless he could be sure of winning it. So, although leaders in Congress kept clamouring for something to happen, he hung on, waiting for the right moment.

In the meantime, Clinton captured several forts on the Hudson River, one of them at Stony Point. On 15 July Washington sent 'Mad Anthony Wayne' with a picked band of men in a silent midnight bayonet attack, to re-take Stony Point. (He got his nickname because he was so reckless.) His soldiers fought, as Wayne wrote to Washington, 'like men determined to be free', and the fort was again in American hands.

After this nothing much happened. The two enemies watched each other keenly, but neither would risk a battle. So the summer passed and in October Clinton moved his troops down to New York for the winter.

On 1 December 1779, Washington rode into winter quarters in Morristown, New Jersey. The winter of 1779–80 was one of 'dreadful extremity'. There were blizzards, thick ice, screaming winds, destitution and hunger, bitter grumblings among the soldiers, and even mutiny. The French furnished uniforms for the American Army, but the rest of the supplies were in a complete turmoil. There were so many shortages that Washington wrote: 'Our affairs are in a more distressed, ruinous and deplorable state than they have been since the commencement of the war.'

One soldier wrote that all he had eaten in four days was a little black birch bark 'which I knaw off' a stick of wood. He saw men roasting their old shoes and eating them!

The snow was still eight inches deep at the end of March. It was a summer of suffering, too. The thirteen states still held their purse strings 'as though they would damn the world rather than part with a dollar to their army'. Washington's troops shrank from 25,000 to 3,000 men. There was so little food that he had to turn militia away.

At one moment Washington was hopeful, for a French fleet arrived. Disappointment again! A larger British fleet prevented the French from attacking. Then the bad news of General Gates's defeat arrived. Finally, came one of the bitterest shocks of all. Major-General Benedict Arnold, the hero of Quebec, Ticonderoga and Saratoga, had turned traitor! This is how General Nathanael Greene's Orders of the Day for 26 September 1780 described Arnold's treachery:

'Treason of the blackest dye was yesterday discovered. General Arnold who commanded at West Point, lost to every *sentiment* of honour and of public and private *obligation*, was about to deliver up that important fort into the hands of the enemy . . . Arnold, the traitor, made his escape to the enemy. Mr André, Adjutant-General of the British Army, who came out as a spy to negotiate the business is our prisoner.'

Major-General Benedict Arnold

Benedict Arnold was a brave soldier, but he had been made bitter by the promotion of younger officers over his head. He was a man who liked to spend money and he had a young and extravagant bride. When he was military governor of Philadelphia, in 1778, he had been dishonest about public property and made money for himself. Congress had questioned his actions and he was *court-martialled* in the winter of 1780.

While the court-martial was pending, Arnold decided, for money, to go over to the British side. He approached Sir Henry Clinton secretly. Arnold's go-between was a china-dealer in Philadelphia who put him in touch with Clinton's adjutant and intelligence officer, Major John André. André and Arnold wrote to each other in code. Arnold sent André military information to pass on to Clinton.

Papers still exist, written by André, that give his ideas on how Arnold could help the British. Clinton, himself, suggested that Arnold should accept a command, 'be surprised and cut off. . . . A service of this nature involving five or six thousand men would be rewarded with twice as many thousand guineas,' Clinton promised.

When the court-martial found Arnold guilty on four of eight counts, and sentenced him to a formal rebuke from Washington, Arnold grew bitterer. He begged Washington to give him command of West Point, the important fortress on the Hudson River. Washington, because of Arnold's brave record, agreed. On 15 July 1780, Arnold wrote Clinton a letter in code offering to sell West Point to the British for £20,000. When, on 3 August, Arnold took command of West Point, his dreams of profitable treason seemed about to be fulfilled.

Arnold arranged for André to come up the Hudson to a secret meeting. There they would make final arrangements for the betrayal. The two men met on the riverbank at midnight on 21 September. Arnold gave André papers to take back to Clinton. They included a map of West Point, information on the fort's *armaments*, summaries of Washington's secret orders—some of them in Arnold's own writing. André hid these papers in his shoes under his stockings.

Arnold was afraid that 'spy boats' on the river might stop André if he tried to return to British lines by the Hudson. He persuaded André to change from his uniform to a claret-coloured coat with gold trim. (Clinton had warned André to keep on his British uniform. Then if he were caught he would be treated as a prisoner of war, not a spy.) Arnold also persuaded André to return by land, and gave him a pass, which Arnold himself signed. André reluctantly took Arnold's advice both in the matter of clothes, and means of going back to New York.

On his way back to safety, André was stopped by three Rebel militiamen. In searching him for money, they found the papers in his shoes. André was taken to the commander of a near-by dragoon detachment. His papers were sent on to Washington. By mistake they first reached Arnold, who was eating his breakfast. After warning his wife, Arnold fled to the 'Vulture', a British warship moored in the Hudson.

Pretty Mrs Arnold's wails and tears convinced Washington's young officers that she must be innocent (although she was really deeply involved in the plot). She also convinced Washington, and was allowed to join her husband in New York.

Mrs. Arnold dressed for a ball.

André was tried and sentenced to hang as a spy. Charles Stedman, the Loyalist historian, said, 'the board of officers fixing their attention upon the naked fact of his being in disguise within their lines . . . were of the opinion that he came under the description and ought to suffer the punishment of a spy.'

André's courage and dignity impressed his American captors deeply. When 'he met his fate like a brave man' there was as much grief in the American camp as in British headquarters. Major André's body now lies in Westminster Abbey, where it was taken after the Revolution.

Arnold reached New York City in safety. He was given over £6,000, a pension for his wife, and was named a brigadier-general, but, as you can imagine, he was very unpopular in the British Army.

West Point was safe. The link between the New England and Middle states was safe. Arnold's treason had failed, but it shocked the men who had trusted him so long. One of his officers wrote: 'Treason, treason! treason! black as h-ll! . . . We were all astonishment, each peeping at his next neighbour to see if any treason was hanging about him.'

A Land Laid Waste

Treachery in the north. Defeat in the south—by October 1780 the Rebel cause had touched its darkest depths. The Government was weak. After six years of war the citizens seemed ready to let their army starve. Money had gone down in value, until Washington said, it took a wagon-load of money to buy a wagon-load of food.

Then on 7 October 1780, at King's Mountain upon a high ridge between South and North Carolina, the Rebels won a battle! Every man on both sides of the battle, except the British commander, Major Patrick Ferguson, was a colonial—Rebel or Loyalist. It was the only battle of the Revolution entirely between Americans.

'Bull Dog' Ferguson was the best rifleman in the British Army. His raids were feared as much as Banastre Tarleton's, so when Cornwallis sent him into the North Carolina backcountry, to organize the Tories there, the Rebel frontiersmen gathered 3,000 strong to drive him out. They pursued him and his 1,000 Tories to high, stony King's Mountain.

Ferguson waited on top of the ridge. The Rebels dismounted, tied up their horses, and pushed, in a light rain, in horseshoe formation, through the sheltering trees. Shooting and re-loading, they fought from tree to tree to the summit. Ferguson, vowing he would 'never yield to such damned bandits', rushed forward, hacking with his sword until he was shot down. Immediately, his men surrendered.

76

With the vengeful shout, 'Tarleton's Quarter! Tarleton's Quarter!' the Rebels killed many of the surrendering Loyalists. The Battle of King's Mountain lasted only an hour. It meant that Cornwallis had to withdraw his troops from North Carolina.

On the same day as King's Mountain, Congress, finally heeding Washington's wishes, replaced General Gates by General Greene. When Greene, with Von Steuben to train his raw troops, reached Charlotte, N.C., in December 1780, he found only 1,500 men fit for duty. (Having won at King's Mountain the militia as usual all went home.) Greene also found he had only enough food for three days, and no money. His army 'was wretched beyond description', Greene wrote, 'so *addicted* to plundering they were a terror to the inhabitants'. He added also, 'Whigs and Tories pursue each other with little less than savage fury.'

General Greene

Since Cornwallis had three men to his two, and the countryside had been laid waste, guerrilla warfare, Greene decided, was his only hope. He sent out Daniel Morgan, the *buckskinned* giant whose riflemen had shot so well at Saratoga. Morgan met Banastre Tarleton with 750 men at Cowpens in South Carolina. It was a bitterly cold morning, 17 January 1781. Tarleton ordered an immediate attack. The first two Rebel lines fell back before Tarleton's onrush. Then, in from either side, Morgan's men closed in a

Lord Cornwallis

bayonet charge. Tarleton lost hundreds in dead, wounded and prisoners. Twelve Rebels were killed, sixty wounded. The Battle of Cowpens, Cornwallis said, 'almost broke my heart.'

Cornwallis was determined to avenge Cowpens. So he set out after the Rebels as fast as he could go. Morgan was too weak to risk another battle. In a 100-mile two-day march, he joined Greene. Cornwallis was so keen to catch Morgan and Greene that he burned most of his supplies, baggage and wagons because they were slowing him up. He burned things he would afterwards need desperately To set an example, he even burned his personal belongings, while his army looked on.

Greene led Cornwallis on a 'country dance', through icy, muddy roads north towards Virginia, then back into North Carolina, into West Virginia, and finally back into North

Carolina. What was left of the British supplies was long since finished by then.

Then on 15 March 1781 (before his militia got restless and went home 'to kiss their wives and sweethearts') Greene picked a battleground and waited for Cornwallis's attack. He chose a place near thickly wooded ground. Since a brick courthouse stood on a near-by hill, the fight was known as the Battle of Guilford Courthouse.

Greene had 4,500 men against Cornwallis's 1,900. Greene arranged his lines as Morgan had at Cowpens. He put his raw troops in the front, telling the men behind them 'to shoot down the first man that runs'. But—alas— once the front row had fired its volleys, it fled. The 'long, obstinate and bloody' battle was after all won by superior British artillery. But one out of every four of Cornwallis's men fell. Charles James Fox, in London, said: 'Another such victory would destroy the British Army.'

Cornwallis's winning army was crippled. He had almost no supplies. He dared not stay inland any longer. He marched to the coast—to Wilmington—where the fleet could supply him with food, etc. But he had no idea what Clinton wanted him to do. On 10 April 1781, Cornwallis wrote to Clinton: 'I am very anxious to receive Your Excellency's commands, being totally in the dark as to the intended operations of the summer.'

On the same day Cornwallis wrote to another British general: 'I am quite tired of marching about the country in quest of adventures.'

If Cornwallis was in the dark about what his commander expected of him, Greene was not. Doggedly he started to destroy the British posts in the interior. In this he was aided by Francis Marion and his guerrillas. Marion had become an almost *legendary* person. He could strike at Tory forces without warning and get away without being caught. Banastre Tarleton named him 'The Swamp Fox', and so he is known in American history. Sometimes he had less than twenty men in his band, sometimes several hundred. Greene used Marion and his men with great success.

Not that Greene was winning battles in the summer of 1781. In fact he lost three battles. Like Washington he lost his battles and won his campaigns. With Marion the Swamp Fox to help him, he could write to the French envoy, 'We fight, get beat, rise and fight again.'

It must never be forgotten that over 5,000 Negroes fought for American independence. They were at Lexington and Bunker Hill. When Washington took command, however, Negroes were forbidden to join the Rebel army. But later, after the English offered freedom to any slave who went into the British Army, Congress lifted its ban. The Rebels desperately needed the help of all able-bodied men.

There were Negroes in the navy. One, a captain from Virginia, was reclaimed by his master after the war and died in slavery. They were effective spies. A double spy brought false information to Cornwallis, true to Lafayette.

More than 100,000 slaves were freed as a direct result of the Revolution. More than 100,000 'voted with their feet' and left the United States for Canada, the West Indies and England after the war. In spite of the part they played, more than 80 years were to pass between the end of the American Revolution and the end of Negro slavery in America.

The World Turned Upside Down

The British generals never seemed able to work together. First it was Burgoyne and Howe who disagreed; now it was Clinton and Cornwallis. Cornwallis believed that winning in Virginia could mean winning the entire war. He wanted Clinton to leave New York and gather the whole British Army together in Virginia. Clinton had 20,000 men idling in New York. But he dared not leave the city, for Washington would pounce in and take it. So the two British commanders disagreed. In May 1781 Cornwallis moved into Virginia and took command of the 7,000 British troops there. After some time he received direct orders from Clinton to move to the coast, establish a base there, and send some of his army up to New York. So he marched down to Yorktown, a small port on the York River, off Chesapeake Bay.

Back in the north, a French land force under General Count Donatien de Rochambeau was working closely with Washington. Rochambeau 'the ideal ally' had placed 4,000 French under Washington's command. He also gave Washington $20,000 from his war chest. But without naval help, de Rochambeau and Washington could do nothing against Clinton's 17,000 men in New York.

Then in August 1781, de Rochambeau heard from Admiral Francois Joseph de Grasse. De Grasse planned to come from the West Indies to Chesapeake Bay later on in the month. His orders allowed him to stay only until the middle of October. Then he must return to the

West Indies to defend the French islands there. Here was Washington's hoped-for chance! If he could get his whole army down to Virginia to attack Yorktown from the land, and de Grasse could attack it from the sea, Cornwallis's army could be destroyed.

A short time before, a letter from Washington to Lafayette inviting him to come north and join in an attack on New York had fallen into British hands. This convinced the British that the Rebels' main aim was to capture New York. Washington had now completely changed his plan, but it was easy to deceive Clinton into thinking that he was still going to attack the city. In fact, he planned a rapid, secret march to Virginia, leaving only 2,000 men behind to hoodwink Clinton in New York. He did not even tell his own men where they were going.

On 15 August 1781, Washington alerted his army of Americans and French: 'General Orders are now issued for the army to prepare for movement at a moment's notice'. By 20 August they were on their way—where to? To New York, they thought, but at Kingsbridge they were ordered to 'right about'. As they marched, the soldiers betted on where they were off to. Most still thought they were making for the New Jersey shore of the Hudson River to aid in a siege of New York. At last, on the twenty-first, they knew! 'We are stealing a march on the enemy,' one of them wrote, 'and are actually destined for Virginia in pursuit of the army under Lord Cornwallis!'

Americans and French marched through Paramus, Springfield and Princeton. Wagons carried their packs so that they could march faster. The army buzzed with rumours—was it true that a French fleet was on its way to help? They crossed Pennsylvania. Marching through Philadelphia their two-mile-long line raised 'dust like a smothering snow'. Then they marched through Maryland

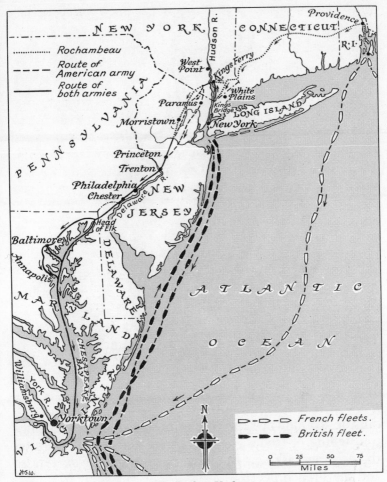

Map labels:
NEW YORK · CONNECTICUT · Providence · R.I. · Hudson R. · West Point · Kings Ferry · White Plains · Paramus · Kings Bridge · LONG ISLAND · Morristown · New York · PENNSYLVANIA · Princeton · Trenton · Philadelphia · Chester · Delaware R. · NEW JERSEY · Head of Elk · DELAWARE · Baltimore · Annapolis · MARYLAND · CHESAPEAKE BAY · ATLANTIC OCEAN · Williamsburg · York R. · Yorktown · VIRGINIA · N

.... Rochambeau
-- -- -- Route of American army
———— Route of both armies

D–D–D French fleets.
▰–▰–▰ British fleet.

0   25   50   75
Miles

The Dash to Yorktown

till they reached the point where boats were ready to carry them down the Chesapeake and up the James River to Williamsburg in Virginia. (Washington was able to go home to Mount Vernon, his great plantation in Virginia, for the first time since 1776.) Lafayette, who was watching

83

The Marquis of Lafayette

outside Yorktown, kept getting messages from Washington, telling of troops, heavy cannon and ammunition on the way, and asking, 'But what has become of de Grasse and the French fleet?'

De Grasse and his fleet were on their way too. He was racing the British admirals, Graves and Hood, to the Chesapeake. He got there first. French ships blocked the James River, preventing Cornwallis from crossing and escaping to the south. French ships sealed off the York River. French ships guarded the mouth of the Chesapeake.

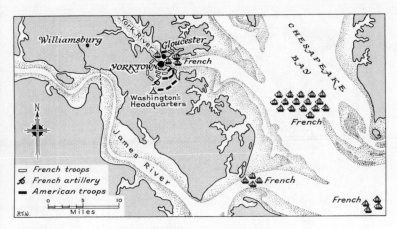

The Siege of British-held Yorktown

Then the French and British fleets met in battle on 5 September 1781. There were twenty-four ships from France, to nineteen British ships. Graves blundered and, before he could correct his error, another French fleet had come up to reinforce de Grasse. Saying 'We cannot *succour* him nor venture to keep the sea any longer', Graves sailed away, leaving Cornwallis without any help from the British Navy.

When the French and Americans arrived outside of Yorktown, between 14 and 24 September, they made a semicircle around Cornwallis's strongly-built defences. The Americans were on the right, the French on the left. The French fleet controlled the bay.

Rebel militia poured into camp as they had poured in at Boston, at Saratoga, King's Mountain and Cowpens. When, on 9 October, Washington touched off the first cannon, 16,000 French and Americans hemmed in Cornwallis's 6,000.

Across the river on the Gloucester Shore, Armand

French soldiers

Louis, Duc de Lauzun (one of the French allies), kept Banastre Tarleton in check.

Washington had one final great worry—would de Grasse stay long enough to complete the siege, long enough to force Yorktown to surrender? On 23 September, a letter came from de Grasse. It told Washington that the French had to leave for the West Indies by 16 October.

Washington wrote back urgently: 'The enterprise against Yorktown under the protection of your ships is as certain as any military operation can be ... and its consequences must necessarily go a great way towards *terminating* the war.'

Washington sent Rochambeau and Lafayette to plead his case. They got de Grasse's promise. He would stay after 15 October, if need be. (Cornwallis actually started to think about surrendering on the seventeenth.)

From 10 to 15 October there was a 'tremendous *incessant* firing from the American and French batteries ... the British ships were wrapped in a torrent of fire ... the bomb-shells from the besiegers and besieged incessantly crossing each other'.

On 16 October, at eleven o'clock at night, Lord Cornwallis made one last try to break out from the trap. He sent the first of three groups of men across the York River at Gloucester Point where the American line was weakest.

They were to fight their way southwards. But a sudden *squall* scattered the boats. When at two o'clock in the morning the storm was over, it was too late to bring the rest of the men across. As Tarleton wrote, 'soon after day-break they returned under the fire of the enemy's batteries to Earl Cornwallis at Yorktown. . . . Thus expired the last hope of the British Army.'

Cornwallis's only chance of rescue was Clinton in New York. But Clinton either could or would not understand his extremity. Not until 17 October (the day surrender negotiations began) did he send troops from New York.

At ten o'clock on that same morning (the second anniversary of Burgoyne's surrender at Saratoga), through the powder and smoke, the Americans heard a beating drum. A little British drummer boy in scarlet had climbed on a parapet. He was beating for a *parley*. A big grenadier officer climbed up beside him waving a white handker-chief. An American officer ran forward from the Rebel lines.

Letters and flags of truce began travelling between Cornwallis's and Washington's headquarters. Before noon on 19 October 'in the trenches before Yorktown' the surrender papers were signed. Washington, and de Rochambeau (de Grasse was ill) put their names to the terms Cornwallis had accepted.

Two o'clock of the same day was the formal surrender hour. The French soldiers in sparkling white, their weapons gleaming, marched to the west of the Hampton Road to Yorktown. The Americans in hunting shirt and buckskin, their worn uniforms of every colour and kind, marched to the east.

General Charles O'Hara of the Guards rode out from the British lines. (Cornwallis, pleading illness, did not appear.) When O'Hara offered his sword to Washington,

Washington said, 'Never from such a good hand', but indicated that O'Hara, a second in command, should surrender to General Lincoln, Washington's second in command.

As the British and Tories laid down their arms and were marched away, their bands played an old melody, 'The World Turned Upside Down'. No one knew it at the time but the last great campaign, the last great battle for American independence, had been fought and won! And General Washington had won it. At the Surrender of Yorktown his six-year-old dream came true. A joint French sea and American land force had decisively defeated the British Army in America. As the poet, Lord Byron, wrote of George Washington: "his was the all cloudless glory to free his country."

The Fate of the Loyalists

'Oh, God, it is all over,' Lord North cried when he heard about Cornwallis's surrender at Yorktown. But it was not all over! Two years passed before the Treaty of Paris ended the Revolution.

In those two years Washington held his hungry and even *mutinous* army together. Fighting in the United States dwindled to a few skirmishes in the south. In those two years England put all her strength into winning at sea. She won so well—against the French in the West Indies and Spanish at Gibraltar—that by 1783 she could have set much stiffer terms than she did.

The Treaty of Paris, signed on 3 September 1783, gave the territory between the Allegheny Mountains and the Mississippi River to the United States. The Canadian–American boundary was much as it is now. Florida went to Spain. Look at the second map inside the front cover.

Some very important questions had to be answered before the Treaty was signed. They concerned the Loyalists. What was to become of them? Must the Rebels give them back the property they had stolen? If the Rebels did not return the property, must they repay the Loyalists for their losses?

To the chief American negotiator, Benjamin Franklin, the Loyalists were America's 'bitterest enemies'. He warned England that if she wanted a peace treaty she had better 'drop all mention of the refugees'. By 1783 England wanted a peace treaty very much. She was sick of the

89

American war. She wanted to end the American–French alliance. The English Government also knew that, without fighting again, it could not force the Americans to repay the Loyalists for their losses.

Richard Oswald, an English negotiator, thought of a *compromise* which Congress accepted. He suggested that Congress should recommend that each State investigate the seizures of Loyalist property and, if they seemed unfair, to correct them.

Who were the Loyalists? What happened to them after the Revolution? The Loyalists (or as their enemies called them, the Tories) were Americans who after the Declaration of Independence in July 1776 wanted America to remain in the British Empire. Certain sorts of people were often Loyalists, such as government officials, lawyers, doctors, Anglican clergymen, large landowners in the north, small landowners in the southern states.

American legend had it that all Loyalists were rich and powerful, people who feared the Revolution would deprive them of their wealth and influence. Historians now know there were Loyalists among all groups, labourers and weavers as well as lawyers and landowners. Negro slaves became Loyalist when England promised them their freedom if they fought in the British Army. Surprisingly, people who were not of English descent were more apt to be Loyalist than those whose ancestors had come from England.

Loyalist strength differed in each colony. They were strong in North Carolina, weak in South Carolina. Weakest in Massachusetts and Virginia, they were very strong in Pennsylvania and New York. If Loyalist New York and Pennsylvania had not been 'put in awe' by strongly Rebel Massachusetts to the north, and Virginia to the south, they well might not have joined the Revolution at all! From the end of 1776 until after the Treaty of 1783 New York City remained in British hands. If the British had not yielded her up peacefully, it would have been almost impossible to get them out by force.

QUEEN's RANGERS.

All young and able-bodied MEN,

[Seafaring Men excepted]

WHO are defirous of ferving their KING and COUNTRY, during the prefent Rebellion, will repair to the Commanding Officer's Quarters of the Queen's Rangers at Kenfington, where they will receive their full Bounty, Cloathing, Arms and Accoutrements

PHILADELPHIA Printed by JAMES HUMPHREYS, Jun
in Market-ftreet, between Front and Second-ftreet

Recruiting Poster for Loyalists

As in all civil wars the American Revolution broke up long friendships and loving families. The Rebel leader Benjamin Franklin never forgave his son William for remaining a Loyalist.

How many Loyalists were there? No one knows exactly, but there were Loyalists in every colony. Probably about one third of all the people who took an active part in the Revolution were loyalists in sympathy.

Why, if there were Loyalists everywhere, and Great Britain's army and navy were behind them, did their side lose? The Loyalists never worked together as well as the Rebels did. They laughed at Sam Adams's Committees of Correspondence but never got together themselves so that

Loyalists in one colony could exchange ideas and news, or even find out who were Loyalists in the other colonies.

Most important: before the Declaration of Independence many Loyalists and Rebels agreed politically on many things. They both resented the King's ministers. They both opposed 'taxation without representation'. They both wanted a restoration of their 'Englishmen's rights'. What they disagreed about was independence itself. The Loyalists feared the 'mob rule' independence might bring far more than they resented Parliament's new taxes.

Since the two parties agreed on so much, the Loyalists were caught off guard when, in July 1776, independence was declared. Suddenly, after 4 July, they were no longer considered law-abiding citizens, but traitors to their native land! And if their wealth and position made them

Loyalist cartoon of Rebels tarring and feathering a tax-collector

the objects of envy, Rebel mobs threatened them with tar
and feathers, so they fled out of the country. Over 50,000
Loyalists fought during the Revolution. The names of
some of their regiments are the British Legion, the King's
Orange Rangers and the Maryland Loyalists.

What became of the Loyalists after the Revolution?

If their position did not excite envy in their neighbours,
if they kept their political opinions to themselves, if they
never fought against the Rebels, they could live quietly,
without being attacked, right through the Revolution and
afterwards. Many of them did, and became leaders in the
young American republic. But if they left the country
during the Revolution or joined the British Army, their
lands and property were confiscated.

Early in the Revolution 1,000 Massachusetts Loyalists
sailed with Howe from Boston to Halifax. Thousands
more migrated later to Nova Scotia and Quebec. They
created the province of New Brunswick. The descendants
of the 60,000 exiles to Canada became very strong there.
They did much to keep Canada in the British Empire and
Commonwealth. Known as United Empire Loyalists, they
have given Canada statesmen, warriors and educators.

Southern Loyalists travelled to the West Indies—
where their heirs have preserved British traditions. The
wealthiest Loyalists went to England. As early as 1775
they were dining together each week at the New England
Club, meeting at the New England Coffee House on
Threadneedle Street in London.

Though many Loyalists felt they had been betrayed,
England generally treated them fairly and generously. By
1782 annual pensions totalling £70,000 were being
awarded to them. After a Royal Commission was set up in
1783 to examine their claims, £3,000,000 more were distri-
buted among them. In addition, £26,000 were given each

Count Rumford

year to Loyalists' widows and children. Settlers in Canada received almost £26,000,000.

After the Revolution some of the Loyalists prospered in England and on the Continent. Among these were the painters Gilbert Stuart and John Singleton Copley. (Copley's son became Lord Chancellor.) James Thompson from Massachusetts was a renowned scientist and inventor, an adviser to the King of Bavaria and a count of the Holy Roman Empire. (He took the title, Count Rumford.)

But many of the 100,000 refugees grew homesick and some managed to go home again. Many more, however, stayed in exile, like all political refugees full of wrongs, dreams and stories of the old days. So numerous were they, one Loyalist wrote: 'There will scarcely be a village in England without some American dust in it by the time we are all laid to rest.'

Why were these Loyalists afraid to go home to America after the Revolution was over and Peace Treaty signed? Why did a man like Washington call them "parricides" (father-murderers)? First, after the Declaration of Independence most Rebels automatically considered all Loyalists traitors to the United States. Second, during the war, Loyalists often had spied for the British Army—on their Rebel friends and relatives. Worse, some Loyalists not only organized the brutal Indian raids along the frontiers, but put on war paint and led them. Also, the savage warfare in the Southern states during the final years of the war (though the Loyalists were no crueller than the Rebels) left long and bitter memories behind.

These are some of the reasons why the Loyalists were resented by Rebels during their lives, and why, for generations afterward, they were condemned in American history and literature.

Few Englishmen—and certainly not George III—wanted to be tyrants or to oppress the colonies. In 1788, after it was all over, George III said this about the Revolution: 'We meant well to the Americans—just to punish them with a few bloody noses, and then make bows for the mutual happiness of the two countries. But want of principle got into the army, want of skill and energy in the First Lord of the Admiralty, and want of unanimity at home. We lost America.'

Englishmen who valued their personal liberty eventually realized that the defeat at Yorktown had really done good because it had checked their country's 'drift towards despotism'. They came to see that the American colonies had not been lost in vain. As Horace Walpole put it: 'Let us save the constitution. If England is free, and America is free, though disunited, the whole world will not be in *vassalage*.' So, after the Revolution, while the new United States was making a new kind of government, England, under the leadership of William Pitt, Lord Chatham's son, became strong once more.

THINGS TO DO

1. Find the following places on a map and then write down the reasons why these places became important in the American Revolution:
   Lexington
   Ticonderoga
   New York
   Saratoga
   Savannah
   Yorktown.

2. Write a speech defending the American colonies after the Boston Tea Party. Then write another arguing that they ought to be treated as rebels.

3. Hold an imaginary session of Parliament in your class and debate the whole question for and against the American colonies as it stood in 1774 or 1775.

4. Write a diary of someone living in Boston during the time from May 1775 to March 1776. You can imagine yourself to be either a Rebel or a Loyalist.

5. The Declaration of Independence is very important to Americans. Discuss whether we have any document in our history which is as important to us.

6. Write in your own words a description of three British generals and three American ones who fought in the American Revolution.

7. Draw your own map to show how Burgoyne's plan would have worked if it had been carried out (see p. 40). You can use the map in this book to help you.

8. Write an argument between a Rebel and a Loyalist, either just after the Declaration of Independence had been signed or at the end of the war.

9. Imagine you are a soldier in Washington's army wintering in Morristown in 1779–80. Write a letter home describing the hardships (see pp. 70–1).

10. Explain, using a map, why a navy was so important in the American Revolution.

11. Find a picture of the United States flag today. How many stars are there? What do they stand for? Find out when the latest ones were added and why.

12. Write a short story or a play about an American family whose members split into Rebels and Loyalists and had various adventures fighting on opposite sides in the war.

13. Find out more about George Washington, Benjamin Franklin, Thomas Jefferson, Lord Chatham, and Edmund Burke. You can use an encyclopedia for this.

14. Were Loyalists right to leave the United States after the war? Debate this in class.

15. If you like painting pictures, here are some good subjects:

The Boston Tea Party (p. 1).

Paul Revere's moonlight ride (p. 10).

The Christmas night crossing of the Delaware (p. 36).

Fort Stanwix flying the new flag (p. 43).

The surrender at Yorktown (p. 87).

GLOSSARY

The meanings of words given here are those used in this book; in a dictionary you will sometimes find other meanings.

abuse: wrong

addicted to: very fond of

agitator: one who goes round stirring up people to rebel

alliance: agreement between two nations who become *allies*

apothecary: chemist

armaments: all kinds of weapons used in war

assault: attack

blizzard: heavy snowstorm with high winds.

to blockade: to stop ships from sailing in and out of port

bombardment: attack by heavy gunfire

buckskinned: wearing shoes and leggings of buckskin (deerskin)

to capitulate: to surrender

Coercive Acts: laws forcing colonists to keep certain harsh rules

to command assent: to make people agree

compromise: agreement in which both sides take less than they wanted

conciliation: the attempt to make enemies into friends

Conciliatory Proposals: suggestions for making up a quarrel

confederation: banding together to help each other

Continental Congress: Parliament for all the American colonies

convoy: ships sailing in a group with warships to guard them

co-ordinating: working together

corrupt: ready to take bribes

courtmartialled: tried by a military court

deficient: lacking

delegates: representatives

deriving: receiving

designing men: schemers for their own advantage

destitution: great poverty

dilemma: difficult choice

diplomat: one who conducts the business of his nation in a foreign country

dismemberment: the act of cutting a body into pieces

disposition: temper

to dissolve: to break

diversionary action: military expedition intended to lead the enemy away from the main target

enlistment: period of time for which a soldier is engaged

exports : goods which a nation sells outside the country

extremity : extremely hard times

fiasco : complete failure

guerrillas : soldiers who fight alone or in small bands, pouncing on the
    enemy from hiding-places at every chance

to harass : to worry someone continually

harmony : agreement

to impel : to force

imports : goods which a country buys from outside

impregnable : impossible to capture

inalienable : not to be taken away

incessant : never stopping

Intolerable Acts : laws which were too harsh to bear

legendary : out of a story

meteor : shooting star

militia : volunteer soldiers, not in regular army

mutinous : rebellious

obligation : duty

to obstruct : to hinder

orator : someone who makes great public speeches

pamphlet : short book

pamphleteer : someone who writes pamphlets

parley : meeting between enemies to discuss a truce or peace

pillory : wooden frame with holes for head and arms in which people
    were fixed for punishment

plantation : large estate on which crops, often cotton, were grown

preamble : introduction

privateer : sea raider

Prohibitory Acts : laws forbidding certain things

Provincial Congress : parliament of a single colony

to quarter : to billet soldiers

quartermaster : army officer who looks after supplies

rabble : disorderly crowd

reconciliation : becoming friends again after a quarrel

redcoat : British soldier (his uniform then was red, not khaki)

redoubt : small fort

to repeal : to abolish

resolution : determination

scythe : long, curved knife with long handle, used for cutting grass

self-evident : so clearly true as not to need proving

sentiment : feeling

sharpshooter : man who is an expert shot with a gun

specious : not really true

squall : violent, short storm of wind

station : position in life

strategic point : vital place to hold against the enemy

to succour : to help

to terminate : to end

Tory : member of the political party corresponding to the Conservatives today

unanimity : agreement by all

unanimously : agreed by all

vassalage : lack of freedom

veteran : soldier who has fought in many campaigns

to wager : to bet

Whig : member of the political party corresponding to the Liberals today

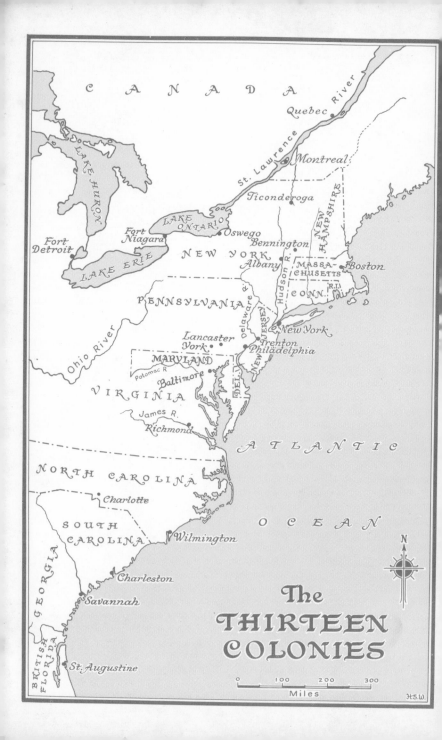

The
THIRTEEN
COLONIES

0   100   200   300
Miles

H.S.W.